# MYSELF THROUGH OTHERS

*Memoirs*

# MYSELF THROUGH OTHERS

*Memoirs*

## DAVID WATMOUGH

DUNDURN PRESS
TORONTO

Editor: Michael Carroll
Copy-editor: Jennifer Gallant
Designer: Jennifer Scott
Printer: Webcom

Library and Archives Canada Cataloguing in Publication

Watmough, David, 1926-
    Myself through others : memoirs / David Watmough.

ISBN 978-1-55002-799-0

    1. Watmough, David, 1926- 2. Watmough, David, 1926- --Friends and associates. 3. Watmough, David, 1926- --Contemporaries.  4. Authors, Canadian (English)--20th century--Biography. 5. Gay authors--Canada--Biography. I. Title.

PS8595.A8Z47 2008      C813'.54      C2008-900715-8

1   2   3   4   5      12   11   10   09   08

 **Conseil des Arts du Canada**  **Canada Council for the Arts**   **ONTARIO ARTS COUNCIL CONSEIL DES ARTS DE L'ONTARIO**

We acknowledge the support of the **Canada Council for the Arts** and the **Ontario Arts Council** for our publishing program. We also acknowledge the financial support of the **Government of Canada** through the **Book Publishing Industry Development Program** and **The Association for the Export of Canadian Books**, and the **Government of Ontario** through the **Ontario Book Publishers Tax Credit** program and the **Ontario Media Development Corporation**.

Printed and bound in Canada

www.dundurn.com

| | | |
|---|---|---|
| Dundurn Press<br>3 Church Street, Suite 500<br>Toronto, Ontario, Canada<br>M5E 1M2 | Gazelle Book Services Limited<br>White Cross Mills<br>High Town, Lancaster, England<br>LA1 4XS | Dundurn Press<br>2250 Military Road<br>Tonawanda, NY U.S.A.<br>14150 |

*To my partner, Floyd, who has shared the chiaroscuro of life with me since we were introduced in Paris fifty-seven years ago*

# CONTENTS

# INTRODUCTION

I should begin by explaining not only the title of this book but what my intention is to write it. It is not an autobiography — and the reasons for that are twofold. First, I do not think I own the skills that pertain to writing interestingly, insightfully, and sustainedly about myself. Second, I have raided my life so often and so extensively on behalf of my fiction that not only am I unsure now what is fact and what is invention but also the skeletal remains are altogether resistant to my probing. Skeletons are not redolent of individuality, save, perhaps, for the pathologist.

On the other hand, I have been blessed since childhood with encounters with an astonishing number of singular people, some of them of high profile, some of them not, but all of them with the power in their personalities to define my own self and to give edge to the qualities that make and shape me. The benison of their impact extends from simply enriching my vocabulary to informing my character and, in some cases, to developing, perhaps, my genetic inheritance of temperament and deportment.

The metaphor I would use for myself in this context is a multi-faceted piece of cut glass that refracts the light from the bright glow of the characters who have strewn the path along which I have stumbled for the past eighty or more years.

There is a darker corollary of course. There are those I've met who were less positive influences, who cast not light but shadow upon my being. I would not go so far as to blame them for a certain contumely I have exhibited from time to time (I believe that and also certain curmudgeonly traits I've exhibited are genetically *inherited*, even if I have not a scrap of scientific evidence to support such a claim). But I have encountered those of ill will who have taught me to be alert in the presence of danger. It is they who through their mischief have inadvertently honed such atavistic instincts to defend and assert myself, my mate, and our kind — and to affirm certain values that seem to wax and wane in popularity over the years. I refer to such demanding challenges as forgiveness, compassion, and noblesse oblige.

Although the terms get bandied about a lot by American presidents and the like, looking back at what of my eight decades I can honestly remember, there have been very few men or women I can characterize as truly good or really evil. I will endeavour to include such in this narrative but the truth is, of course, that the vast majority of us tramp along that grey equator of moral life — even if we are cribbed and confined by other versions of human extremity such as cruelty and vindictiveness.

But of such matters I knew nothing as a child growing up — not until my seventeenth year, when I was thrown into jail by mendacious police in Portsmouth, England, and found guilty by the magistrates and sent to Winchester Prison for "Soliciting and Importuning." Before then was a quasi-idyllic childhood and youth that I only later could perceive as rather odd.

Although born in 1926 in the London borough of Leyton and transported within a year or so to a quiet street decorated with silver birches in South Woodford, a leafy, outer suburb on the fringes of Epping Forest, it wasn't very long before I began a parallel existence in the place of my father's ancestry that could not have been more different. That was North Cornwall, and the village of St. Kew, where my paternal line had been yeoman farmers for centuries and, indeed, was centuries as well as four hundred miles apart from the upper-middle-class suburb that was the parliamentary constituency of Winston Churchill.

The Cornwall to which I returned annually until the outbreak of war, and from then on through the war years lived with my aunt who was also my godmother on the family farm, was another world from London E18. In Cornwall we fetched water from a well, had no electricity and no telephone, and young and middle-aged men rode bicycles (the elderly still used a pony and trap) to the nearest town, Wadebridge, more than four miles away, to fetch freshly charged accumulators for our battery-run radios.

Perhaps most looming for a young boy (though I am now inclined to think it is relevant to most of us) was "the toilet situation." In Cheyne Avenue it was all so simple. If you wanted to do your business you simply defecated, wiped your bottom, and pulled the chain. Cornwall presented a far more hazardous affair — not least for a prudish child such as me. On our farm, for instance, "number two" demanded a trip across the farm-yard and down an orchard before encountering the slate-built outhouse. And that walk itself entailed the risk of confronting an irate gander who guarded his geese by half opening his wings, loudly hissing, and making short runs at you. My lewd cousin had taught me that the object of the gander's spite was that small part of me that resembled a worm — which he insisted, quite unscientifically, was the staple of a goosey gander. There was also an old, human-hating rooster who lay in wait for the unwary down the narrow path that itself was redeemed at least in the spring by a profusion of wild daffodils.

Then, when you were inside the cramped, whitewashed space, there were other alien demands and factors. There was the smell alone, which, although tamed by the powdered lime that one had been taught to scat-ter down the open hole when finished, was still an offence to cosseted suburban nostrils. That problem would disappear after a few days' ac-climatization back on the farm, but there were other matters that refused such accommodation.

The hard wooden bench with its two circular holes (ours was a two-seater, though I have no recollection of both seats being used simultane-ously) was rough on the buttocks. But even rougher was the wad of torn-up newspaper on a rusty nail that served as toilet paper. I never did really get used to that.

There were other Cornish lavatories in my youthful memory that, if not presenting hazards from geese and farmyard fowls, did certainly present em-barrassment from an avian source. One such was at my Great-Aunt E.A.'s house in Pendoggett. Ancient (eighty-four) Great-Aunt E.A. (for Elizabeth Anne), who dressed entirely in black widow's weeds and who had gums where others had teeth and would cheerfully munch hardtack and offer

11

us children bananas while herself eating their skins, had her lav at the very back of her house. To reach it entailed first going down a long slate corridor to an open porch overlooking a distant Atlantic. There to the left stood the desired place. Initially relieved that I'd made the distance without accident (at least on the farm you could squat in the orchard if things became desperate), I would sit down, again on rough wood, and start to exert myself.

But Great-Aunt E.A. never disclosed that she put her broody hens in there to sit on their eggs until hatched — so that you'd never know until too late what state of evolution the eggs had reached. Sometimes there was just warning clucking, and sometimes chirruping as little yellow balls of chicks scurried over your sandals, and always there was the loud squawking of zealous mother hens frequently accompanied by an angry peck at bare legs as you were warned that you were trespassing on their maternal space. It is perhaps understandable that the first days back in my Cornish paradise were often sullied by an enforced constipation.

However, upcountry in our Woodford home we had not only all such "mod cons" as flush WCs and enamelled bathtubs in bathrooms, and electric fires as well as coal and radiators, but by the late 1930s most of those in Cheyne Avenue owned cars and telephones and received regular television programming from the BBC.

My maternal grandfather had one of the first telephones in the kingdom and owned a double-fronted house flanked by Landseer-type lions along the Leyton High Road. But more than that, he had money from his real-estate ventures in the East End of London. In the middle-class sense, the Bassetts were more than comfortably off. There were numerous maids, if no menservants, and holidays abroad in the days before common citizens needed passports.

My father's family were correspondingly only "land rich," inheriting farms rarely more than one hundred acres, and somewhat short on that convenient constituent of exchange that my mother used to jokingly refer to as "spondulicks" — a Victorian term for money that I think she picked up from her father's tenants. Then my mother was in love with everything Victorian — from manners and mores to morality.

I was blessed with excellent parents and my love for each of them was equal. So it is not a matter of imbalance in that quarter that made me so early in my existence feel the tug of Cornwall as infinitely the stronger and informing force. My bourgeois Woodford years, which lasted until I was thirteen, are not much more than a blur, but my Cornish memories from the yeoman side of our family are vivid and multiple from the age of four or five.

A curious affirmation of that arose when my East London–based school, the Coopers' Company School, was evacuated in 1940 to Frome in Somerset. I had been living in Cornwall with the younger of my two brothers since the outbreak of the war and thus separated from my parents, who had returned to London where my mother was to become a wartime ambulance driver and my father her "boss" when he ran a first-aid post for the Civil Defence.

On arriving in Somerset from my Cornish home I immediately compared adversely the natural artifacts of that English county to those of the Celtic Duchy. The hedges were "wrong" (not being built with stones of granite and reinforced with slate); farm animals looked alien. The cows were too small and the chickens were of unfamiliar breeds; indeed, the lengthy, short-turfed fields were themselves heretical to my teenage eyes. And a subsequent brief spell in next-door Wiltshire sustained the Cornish superiority in all these rustic things. It was at school, I think, where I first realized that, London connection and my mother's family notwithstanding, I was an ardent Cornishman.

And that has been undying — even after a successful and happy transplant and my subsequent rerooting as a proud Canadian. Unlike some North American immigrants I am happy with a prefix. Not only that, but a vivid awareness of my Cornish background has given me an objectivity when regarding the English that I think North Americans appreciate. The source of that was the Celtic liberation from the rigid class-consciousness that manacled and blinkered so many Britons of my generation. I spoke with two accents — Cornish dialect and BBC English — and never felt a sense of class-consciousness via the tongue as did so many of my social peers in the United Kingdom.

Fortunately, too, my school, founded in 1535 by the London Guild of Coopers (barrel makers), was egalitarian, housing poor scholarship boys from the East End, many Jewish boys from Mile End and Bethnal Green, and boys whose forebears had also attended Coopers' over generations, some of whom were wealthy enough in the late 1930s to drive to school in their own cars — even though the headmaster frowned on the practice. My father was devoid of any social consciousness; not so my mother.

Cornwall also taught me the inner meaning of colonialism, and although I have never allied myself with the political left it has given me a sense of *blutbrüderschaft* with all subject peoples of every colour and gender. I thank the Duchy for saving me from racial and class prejudices. The English, who were welcomed each summer as middle-class holidaymakers by all of us for their money if not their accents, were called "emmets" behind their backs — "emmet" being a Celtic word for "ant," and in this context a distinctly pejorative kind of ant at that! I wholly understood the instinct. By extension, I have always felt affinity for places and countries that are sustained by the tourist trade.

It is perhaps not surprising that the first folk to radically illumine my sensibilities and spark wonder in me inhabited the farms, villages, and hamlets I first knew and through which I herded sheep on their way to being "dipped" against parasites, cows brought in from the fields for milking, and the gentle giant farm horses I rode bareback as a ten-year-old when taking them to be reshoed by either Mr. Grill's smithy in Pendoggett or another blacksmith further away in St. Tudy.

There was perhaps yet one more factor that secured the North Cornwall of my childhood as the pre-eminent influence in the forming of *who* I thought I was and *what* I thought I was. This was the sheer beauty of my surroundings. Not only was Tipton farm nestled at the foot of an elm-bordered lane, picturesque to an extreme, but St. Kew village, with its Norman, lichen-furred church, was a place of indubitable charm. And my boyhood borders were the vast and mysterious moors just a little to the north and the majesty of the North Atlantic but a mile or so to the west.

And all this nigh-overpowering lure of scenery was further reinforced by the tie of Cornish kinship: I had the claim of cousins and second cousins and their families scattered from De Lank on Bodmin Moor itself to Callington, down the peninsula to St. Columb Major, and finally down to the even milder climes of the port town of Falmouth, where another bevy of Bryants shared kinship as well as holiday revels each summer.

Though I cannot say London had no impact on me at all. Apart from my school being just off the Mile End Road — so that I was able to witness Communist and Fascist marches and the elaborate funeral processions of the East End dead — my parents ensured I visited, and frequently, such places as the Tower, Parliament, the great department stores, the royal palaces, especially Hampton Court, and above all, my favourite, the London Zoo in Regent's Park, which, as members, we were able to visit on Sundays when the crowds were absent.

But I can best sum up my attitude to the metropolis through an exchange I had with one of my professors, later at King's College along the Strand. He was from Ipswich and proud of his East Anglia roots. Yet one day he said, "David, I have now been living here in London for four years and I still cannot for a moment get over the excitement of being in this great city."

I was silent. I realized then for the first time the significance of being born there. I just took all it offered and signified for granted. I believe you can't be more of a Londoner than that. By some odd legal quirk an inheritance of the Freedom of the City of London can be transferred through the female line. We three brothers could have received it through our mother. None of us did.

A caution. Throughout these chapters I provide anecdotes and illustrations of myself and my subjects and I must stress these are intensely personal and thus shaped by my subjectivity and the strength and frailty of memory at different periods in life. I have done my best to adhere to Polonius's advice in *Hamlet*: "This above all: to thine own self be true." All of us perceive events through our own eyes, from our own perspectives, and they can result in astonishingly different versions. This is not objective history (if such exists), but I have striven mightily to make it honest.

# 1
# VILLAGE QUARTET

My very first sense of magic was sparked not by fairy tales and folklore but by Mr. William Lightfoot, a short and Cornishly swart man who invariably wore a bowler hat and a large moustache with bushy eyebrows to match. He and his wife lived in an isolated cottage next to the embankment of the Southern Railway's branch line to Padstow, where wild strawberries grew, and next to a bridge that was laced with mistletoe.

I never went inside his home, which, incidentally, was covered on the outside with roses and was made even more picturesque and "English country garden" (a distinct rarity in rude granite and slate Cornwall) by masses of lupine, delphinium, roses, and peonies and lush hedges of fuchsia and rhododendron.

I know nothing more about Mr. Lightfoot than that he had a squat and bonneted wife who emerged from the cottage even more rarely than he did and that, as there were no apparent children, no sign of a dog, an eerie quiet hung over his dwelling. The aura of that plus his outlandish clothes made me quicken my steps when I walked past his gate or pedal more quickly if I were on the farm bike delivering milk to my great-aunt's house opposite, which was the dower house in our family and to which my parents eventually succeeded.

It was Mr. Lightfoot's practice to stand for hours at his garden gate and make comments to any pedestrian coming from the scattering of cottages forming St. Kew Highway and the turnpike leading south to Wadebridge and proceeding down the lane that led either to our farm and the yet more isolated hamlet of Trequite or down to the pretty village of St. Kew with its Norman church, cobble-fronted Cornish Arms, and Celtic Cross War Memorial above a trout-filled stream.

He was most likely to see me and my cousin Robert when we were off on mid-Sunday morning to Highway Methodist Chapel to be bored by lusty hymn-singing and even more boring sermonizing from a lay preacher. It had become our practice, at least on sunny days, to ameliorate all that boredom by catching a lizard basking on the slate of one of the hedgerows and playing with her (the females were the largest and the ones we aimed for), naming her, etc., as we sat in chapel, striving not always successfully to hide our new pet from Christian eyes.

On the Sabbath morn I have in mind I had caught a particularly large (say eighteen inches long) lizard with a greenish hue that I immediately named Mabel after my godmother — though I did not propose to tell her. Mabel performed admirably in chapel and I was minded to take her also to church that evening for evensong when I sang in the choir. Perhaps I should explain that my dual life already noted was echoed again when back in Cornwall owing to a Methodist uncle who had married my Church of England aunty. Thus I suffered the worship of both denominations with the only limited bonus of an annual Sunday school outing by both parties. Looking back, it is nothing short of amazing that I clung to my Anglican background and in due course became a full-blooded Anglo-Catholic and read theology with the notion of priesthood when I duly attended university.

We had walked with our lizards from "Zig-Zag" Chapel, comparing notes on our reptiles and planning their futures, when we approached Mr. Lightfoot's cottage. He was standing there as usual, his bowler hat tilted over his eyes as we drew before him. The hat wasn't tilted enough to obscure his sight, though. He saw my beauty before I had time to slip her from my palm into my pocket.

"What's that, then? Oi'll tell 'ee what 'tis. That there's a four-legged emmet, boy. Now you be bravun careful. They'll spit poison as soon as look at 'ee. Bewitched buggers they be. Got 'em 'ere in the hedge till I learned how to spell 'em out! Let of 'un go, boy! I bide they do cast their spell particular on tiny tackers like you be."

I had the notion that Mr. Lightfoot had his own spell mechanisms — anyway, I wasn't prepared to risk it. Though it was still with enormous reluctance, I conceded to his force and allowed Mabel to slither off my palm and make her way towards the railway bridge with its veins of mistletoe.

With William John Pearce it was again utterance rather than appearance that inserted itself into a deep niche in my memory. He certainly believed in four-legged emmets and was probably the only person in our village who didn't think Cornish piskies were now just a tourist gimmick. He lived with his sister "up village." She was only known as Miss Pearce and I never learned her other names. Nor did I ever see her more than a few feet from her open stove at seven o'clock when I delivered their milk each morning. And that goes for sweltering days in mid-August as well as in the cooler dark of winter. I saw William John (as only his peers were allowed to call him) on September 3, 1939, when we came out of Zig-Zag Chapel where the preacher had announced the outbreak of the Second World War and told us how sad the prime minister, Mr. Neville Chamberlain, was about it in his radio broadcast. He also made reference to some service at the church of St. Martin-in-the-Fields that held me in good stead when William John informed us young worshippers-about-to-become-lizard-hunters that "Mr. Martin was preaching in them fields that same Sunday — and what's more boy-os, not in no Methody fields neither!"

William John's ecclesiastical ignorance may well have been compounded by the fact that he never saw London in his lifetime and it was said that he never went any further than Wadebridge, which was just four miles away. He knew my great-grandfather and always referred to my father as "young Gerald." He called me "Maister Davey."

He was invariably in attendance at all the farms during their autumn threshing times, when he helped send the stacked wheat through the steam-powered threshing machine, and when working for my uncle he became my mentor. Although living in the Methodist part of our bifurcated village, he was a staunch churchman, and as he showed me how to pitchfork the sheaves between us he also sought to dissuade me from attending Zig-Zag "wi' all they Methodies and their bloody singin'!" He also taught me to deal with the countless rats that had made the cornmow their home since harvest time in August and that threatened to shin up our legs as they panicked when the mow got progressively lower. As one fat and furry malevolence disappeared up his corduroy trouser leg, his browned and gnarled hand came down and tightened around his own leg as he crushed the struggling lump to death. I was rocking with fear and was as grey as granite but he butted me with his free arm. "You b'ain't got nothing to worry about boy-o — not wearing long uns and that. And if one did climb up beyond they bare knees Oi should let of 'un go, 'cos could easy be your own balls and not ole ratty you'd be squeezin'!"

Mrs. Menheniot lived in the sagging-roofed cottages behind St. Kew Church. She was among the village poor. I think her husband was a laid-off labourer who had worked for the Council maintaining the roads. Anyway, they had a swarm of children, many of them red-haired and Celtic-looking, and received our cheapest milk, both separated from all its cream and buttermilk, which was the residue from the butter when we had made it. I brought a bottle of each to her every morning on the milk bike in straw baskets that we called "frails." It was from this daily milk round, incidentally, that I became familiar in puberty, if not before, of the differences in wealth between families and what a difference it made to the dairy products they could afford.

Back in Woodford, of course, we were wholly sealed from either the plight or good fortune of others, as total privacy was the banner of the middle classes. We were somewhat leery of learning the surnames of neighbours, let alone their Christian names. Most residents of Cheyne Avenue were referred to as Mrs. #12 or Mr. and Mrs. End House. Or, failing that, by the breed or name of their dog, as everyone had one.

But it wasn't Mrs. Menheniot's poverty that held my teenage attention so much as the rasp and range of her tongue. Only at one other time — in New Haven, Connecticut, with an Italian countess — have I met a woman of comparable knowledge of male intimacy and an urge to declare it that could devastate me. Mrs. Menheniot naturally addressed me in a strong local dialect — to which I strove to respond in kind, even as cheeks blushed and I tingled hot at her surefire insights. Conversations went rather like what follows.

"Mornin' Missus, quart of separated today, idnun?"

"I moind it be. Bravun more than you did milk from your sel'n in bed last noight I reckon!"

"Did 'ee want buttermilk tomorrow? We'll have it by then as today is butter day. Aunty said as you can have it on tick but to remoind 'ee that you b'aint paid last week's bill yet."

She ignored the financial talk and returned to me. "You had that han'some cousin o' yours yet, then? He were aroun' wi' the milk yesterday and I moind he got gurt great ball's on 'im. Ealier developer that one! And I do know you'm as thick as thieves. I wouldn' loike to be washin' they sheets from the beds you two boys do sleep on. Mrs. Trethewey do say they'm as thick as boards when she do come to do the wash up the farm."

"I gotta be going, Mrs. Menheniot — brave lot more on me round, you! Abyssinia!"

But she wasn't finished. I was back on the heavy milk bike — lady's style without a crossbar — and she was still throwing her darts, only always with a smile and at least leavened by her remark one time that she'd never tell my aunt or uncle (whom she despised) what passed between the two of us.

"I seed 'ee, Davey, hanging round that Ed Chaloe down Wadebridge market. You best be careful wid 'ee, my lad, they say he's a wild one and as rough with the boys as he be with the maids. Now you keep your little pecker from the loikes on 'ee. 'Tis safer in your own hands, Davey, you mark my words."

I did — and for a long time. But the milk round remained a constant and my blushes return even as I remember and write.

I am emotionally indebted to Oliver Dyer, who today would doubtless receive a lengthy prison term as a pedophile and a corrupter of youthful morals, and who in the restrictions of his time was something of a racist, certainly a snob, and, like multitudes of others, a religious hypocrite. Nevertheless I learned more from him in my teens and into early adolescence than from anyone else. I count him as one of the imperishable blessings I have received in this life.

I guess all that needs a little explaining. Oliver was my first local encounter with the gay glue that sometimes seemed to be what stuck the British Raj together. In this case it was a Cornish emigrant. The turn of the century saw him in both India (during a durbar) and South Africa, to where he had initially immigrated. He told me wild tales of liveried Indian servants being felt up by the diners as they stood behind the guests' chairs during formal banquets, of pederasty at every rung of the imperial bureaucracy.

He described wild orgies (a favourite word of his) in the context of the South African Railways, where apparently he was some kind of overseer. Those parties, he said, were truly erotically mixed, involving even race-conscious Afrikaners as well as gay British and various African tribes like the well-endowed Zulu and some Sotho, Tswana, and Xhosa peoples. He gleefully described his own participation in these fleshly revels and loved naming dignitaries utterly unknown to me but who patently fed the world of gossip and scandal he had vacated eventually at the death of his father to return to Cornwall and tend an ailing mother.

She had lasted many years longer than he had anticipated, and he became for twenty years or more the familiar figure of a devoted son, living in the rambling and extensive cottage at the foot of the steep hill between the hamlets of Amble and Tredrizzick. His ample home was most conveniently placed for certain activities that he had brought home with him from the colonies, as schoolboys cycling home in the direction of St. Kew would have to dismount right outside his side entrance in the whitewashed stone of his house. As often as not, he would be standing there in his white ducks and invite them in for tea. They frequently accepted, he said, not for the tea per se, but for the delicious saffron buns he'd baked and the homemade apple and peach pies he also offered hungry young appetites.

A further appeal was the fact that Oliver had a modern bath, the water for which was furnished by a well and heated by a small electric generator fuelled by a windmill in his upper garden. As none of the young men had such an installation, a plentiful supply of them was only too happy to take advantage of his invitation to use his faculties. Among them was a young man who worked on the railway in Wadebridge, and it was through him that I experienced one particular sexual involvement with the retired colonial official.

I was sitting with him in his fern-festooned porch, listening to his exotic as well as erotic stories, when his ever-questing eye spied a youthful figure dismount from his bike, moments before he knocked timidly on the side door. "That's Jan Nankivel," Oliver said in his strange, almost guttural voice that only intermittently held a trace of Cornish. He gave me a playful punch as he got up from his wicker armchair. "He's a stunner, Davey. And if you behave with me I'll let you go up and do his back when he's taking his bath."

The minute I saw the tall and scowling Jan I jumped at the chance. I had seen him on the platform at Wadebridge station and watched him shovelling coal on the locomotive that took the two railway cars between Padstow and Bodmin — a line, incidentally, that was the second oldest in Great Britain. I had long lusted after that lithe body, indeed would have personally licked him clean of coal dust had I been so invited!

Our greetings were no more than a grunt, as he was obviously embarrassed by my presence. I sat there alone while Oliver took his guest upstairs and I heard the running of water. On his return my host explained the procedure I was to follow. He also explained that the price of my activity would be his opportunity to fellate me. One more time of letting him suck my cock didn't bother me. I had even gotten used to the small shock of watching him take out his false teeth and place them in a tumbler of water while he explained that it was to make the experience for me even more pleasant.

Oliver looked at his gold fob watch before giving me the signal to rise and go to Jan Nankivel. When I got to the bathroom, from which steam was faintly curling, I knocked timidly on the partially closed door. I was decidedly nervous and wished Oliver had accompanied me. I heard a splash and thought I heard a grunt. As I entered Jan turned a glistening wet head towards me. I could see more of him below the far from sudsy surface of the water. I almost swooned, maybe would have done had he not barked, "What the hell be you 'ere for?"

"Oliver is busy getting us tea," I gulped. "He asked me to come instead and do your back. May ... may I?"

He didn't answer but merely stood up, facing away from me — revealing his dripping buttocks, coal-dust-flecked spine, and muscular back. I simply approached, picked up the toilet brush in the container hanging over the tub, and began to work delicately across his skin. Only very slowly and gingerly did I take my gentle scrubbing activity beyond where I could see towards his more intriguing front. I needn't have worried. As he slowly turned towards me the very first thing I saw, of course, was his gradually stiffening member. But the next thing I heard was no invitation from Jan Nankivel but a guffaw behind me from Oliver Dyer.

The interruption was cunningly intended to thwart any possibility of my being sexually exhausted before Oliver had had his turn — but all that didn't dawn on me until much later and I was a little more cognizant of human motives. In any case, Jan's angry embarrassment, my own shame, and Oliver's cheerful remarks about the obvious drowned out all such speculation.

Afterwards I let Oliver do what he wanted but even a little worm can turn. I never complied again. Even so, I did continue to see him and thirst upon his gay knowledge and observations.

The very last time we met, though, was in utterly different circumstances. The family was emerging from evensong in our lichen-encrusted Norman church one blithe summer evening when bats from the ancient rafters of the porch flitted and twittered and the first fingers of darkness encircled the graves of great-aunts and great-uncles, of my grandmother and scores of relatives from other centuries whom I would know only by their granite headstones.

We were walking past the sixteenth-century stocks of worm-holed oak that stood as a reminder of responses to criminal acts in another age when Oliver caught us up. He immediately doffed the pith helmet that he had only just put on in coming out of church and addressed my mother. "Mrs.

Watmough," he began, "I have been meaning to tell you this for some time. You will never die while this son of yours lives. He is indeed your happy image." With that he turned, raised his pith helmet again, and was gone.

"What a nice thing for him to say," my mother said.

But my aunt, who was also with the family party, said, "I don't trust that man. He's from Tredrizzick, isn't he?"

But then my father's sister was Cornish and my mother was not.

# 2
# JAN SHENTON, PARISH PRIEST

The Reverend Jan Shenton is not one of my high-profile cameos. Indeed, I doubt whether his name caused even a rustle throughout his ministry in the Diocese of Truro in which he laboured as the vicar of St. Kew all my childhood and youth.

He wasn't a good preacher — in fact he was rather a lousy one, having a flat, monotone voice that easily induced somnolence in his rural and work-tired congregation. He was, though, diligent in visiting both the hamlets and outlying farms in his parish, which was geographically the largest in Cornwall. Ostensibly the reason for his visits was to bring the parish leaflet but that in fact was his mainstay, as he was virtually incapable of small talk and often ill at ease.

Nevertheless, this man was a marked influence on my early life. He was de facto scoutmaster for the village and thus saw me through both Cubs and Boy Scouts and taught me the rudiments as demanded by Lord Baden-Powell. There was no intimacy with us boys — and certainly nothing of the sexual overtones beloved these days of the prurient. But when I took a baby bat, rescued from the ancient rafters of the church porch with the aid of an umbrella's handle, and stroked it during evensong, he obviously noted the activity when he mounted the pulpit to preach. When the service was over, rather than scold me, he fumbled beneath his surplice and came up surprisingly with a fountain pen filler, which he offered me — suggesting that I fill it with milk for the ugly yet beautiful little creature nestled in my hand.

Then it was Jan Shenton who fostered and directed my growing passion to rescue and nurture the various orphan wild animals that increasingly came my way as my reputation as a foster mother of Nature's young grew ever wider. I managed to successfully raise a variety of creatures — from a badger and two fox cubs to a raven, a buzzard, baby ferrets, many grass snakes, and of course lizards.

Another constituent of this parish priest that I think has thoroughly informed my attitudes and thinking was his goodness. He was not a saint. Wasn't in fact a particularly pious man. But in his simple, rather inarticulate way, he loved humanity and knew a real and palpable content when he was serving his parishioners.

By the time I was thirteen I had been exposed to Anglo-Catholic worship and belief in the little church of St. Peter's-in-the-Forest that served our Woodford home and where my parents made their Communion, like so many rudimentary Anglicans, only at Easter. But I attended Mass each Sunday and felt a distinct liturgical bump when I returned to Cornwall and Low Church St. Kew.

It very soon became obvious to me at that time that theologically Mr. Shenton and I stood poles apart. Perhaps only the broad-roofed Church of England could allow such divergence as existed between us. I practised the rosary and regular sacramental Confession — which I am sure was utterly alien to him. In the full flood of teenage religiosity I bobbed my head at the name of Jesus during every church service, genuflected at Mass and before the Blessed Sacrament wherever I confronted it. In the tabernacle of St. Kew Church, after a High Church predecessor had had it inserted on the high altar, Mr. Shenton kept a can of Brasso cleaner.

Yet I can never remember a harsh or dismissive word from him over my admittedly ostentatious practices — and, equally, he never evoked anger or contempt in my heart. And from those small, personal beginnings I learned to respect and love those whose Christianity was remote from mine — which is often harder to accomplish than to achieve a loving respect for those of other faiths altogether such as Muslims and Jews, many of whom I today claim as intimate and beloved friends.

There was yet another appetite that this Anglican priest sparked in me, but in this context he was more a distinct voice amid a number of others.

It was the urge to travel and particularly to explore the terrain of the North American continent. Oddly enough, this came about partly in opposition to the vicar's excessively genteel wife, who was from the neighbouring county of Devon, loathed Cornwall, and mildly disapproved of me.

It was at the annual village fete held on the Feast of St. James the Apostle on July 25 that I once suggested on the crowded if spacious vicarage lawn that on leaving school I might become a veterinarian there in North Cornwall, and Mrs. Shenton at once protested — though in the soft-voiced way that she invariably used. She said I should get right out of Cornwall, attend Oxford or Cambridge, of course, and then think of being a vet in the Home Counties — or at least somewhere, she implied, where civilization was at hand rather than in that primitive neck of the woods.

Her husband took a different tack. "You're Cornish, Davey," he said. "You belong to a race of emigrants. Why not try the Dominions? I think your father said, last time he was down here from London, that he had relatives in Pittsburgh in the U.S. and that his own sister had married and was now in the Australian outback. But if I were you, Davey, I'd head for Canada. The Prairies, maybe ... a city like Winnipeg?"

I'd been expecting that. Half of his sermons led quickly from the Bible to his reminiscing of homesteading days when his dad had farmed in northern Manitoba before eventually going down to the great prairie city between the Red River and the Assiniboine.

I have always reckoned that it was that village fete and the Reverend Jan Shenton's words to me that turned my adolescent compass towards Canada, the eldest daughter of the British Empire, and in a westerly direction at least to the Rockies, if not further. Only it wasn't as a veterinarian that I was eventually to make that journey but as a still unfocused writer.

# 3
# NATALIE GUTHRIE

An even more powerful force in guiding my geographic destiny was a woman who came in wartime to Cornwall to live when she couldn't get back to her home in British Columbia. A middle-aged woman, handsome rather than beautiful, she rented an isolated cottage that stood at the end of a long driveway, the entrance of which faced the solitary house of a widow-farmer who had been my Great-Aunt E.A.'s best friend.

Natalie had quickly become a friend (she was a gregarious woman) of Mrs. Harris's daughter, Cissy, and as soon as the gossip spread around the village of her kindness to spinster Cissy, who had unfortunately become her mother's drudge, I was keen to meet her.

By our local standards she obviously had some money, and maybe the romance of that plus her North American accent appealed to me. In any case, by being a friend to Cissy she was destined to be my friend too. Cissy's dad had been killed in the Great War and her mother had taken over the farm and worked it — making her a unique woman. My dad had told me that in the early days of her widowhood, loud guffaws and sniggers would come from those clustering at the gates of her fields as the diminutive figure in enormous boots and hem-frayed skirts worked her horses at ploughing time, called her cattle in for milking, or did the numerous other chores traditionally reserved for men. I guess she was an early feminist.

But there was a darker side to my great-aunt's friend and neighbour. From 1916 until her death forty years later, their bedroom remained exactly as her husband had left it on his final coffin'd return from the muddy slaughter of the Somme. With my own wide eyes I had seen the opened and fading packet of Woodbine cigarettes on the dressing table where he had left them on his last leave, his serge blue suit and collarless shirts carefully preserved in the great walnut closet and draped across the backs of several chairs. His polished Sunday shoes were at the foot of the brass bed. Cissy had seen that the room was cleaned and dusted — there was no Miss Faversham aspect — but it was a mausoleum nevertheless. And the atmosphere that remained in that house of two lonely women was undoubtedly one of death.

And it was into that that Natalie Guthrie charged in her ebullient way. Not that she trespassed on the room of unhealed grief, but she joked and joshed until Cissy smiled and her mother grinned. I was no longer delivering milk but when I called along with my father, who dutifully regarded Mrs. Harris and her daughter as a special charge arising from his own bloody First World War experiences and his shared links with them of his beloved aunt, it was to find after Natalie's advent a certain lifting of a sombre mood and the two women anxious to regale Father with stories of the newcomer to the village.

I have forgotten the precise chronology, but it was shortly after that I met the only person, beyond family, I was to know both in my Cornish village and then subsequently in Victoria, British Columbia.

She was related, through her marriage, to Tyrone Guthrie of Shakespeare at Stratford, Ontario, fame, and her brother was a headmaster at the Shawnigan Lake School in British Columbia. Part of her earlier life had been in San Francisco, where she had been attached to the staff of the Canadian Consul General, I believe. But all this data should be taken with a pinch of salt, as Natalie's manner of conveying information was in short staccato sentences that she was disinclined to repeat. So you got it the first time or not at all. And woe betide the person who asked for repetition!

This peremptory aspect of her may have been reserved for such as young me — indeed, she did seem to talk otherwise with my father, whom I secretly thought she found sexually attractive. And she used another idiom entirely when conversing with my mother, with whom she certainly did become steadfast chums, both there in Cornwall and London and again in Victoria where Natalie returned to live and die.

I think I was surrogate for one of her own three children, one of whom, Bob, was away fighting in Burma with Brigadier Orde Wingate (who organized the Chindits in guerrilla warfare against the Japanese) and ended up as a humble driving inspector in Vancouver, British Columbia. Another, her eldest daughter, was an officer in the U.S. WAVES in Washington, D.C., and the third and youngest, her "Benjamina," served as a Wren in the Royal Navy, somewhere in England.

At any rate, Natalie set her mind to instructing me for life's challenges and, although much of it passed over my curly head like water, a few of her admonitions remained and did their work. One of these that hit home was the result, I think, of being a rather vain child. I was quite pretty, as boys go, and from an early age had a definite sense of what clothes I liked and what I wanted to wear.

I must have hinted at my sartorial penchant in one way or other, for as I sat there in her mildly "Americanized" Cornish cottage (she regularly opened its sash windows and lit her oil lamps in the daytime if the day was dark) she suddenly asked me to observe her own outfit. "You will see, Davey," she observed, "that my clothes are modest. My outdoor wear is also. The point, young man, is that I am a world traveller and I learned long ago that everything is a matter of choices. If I owned a fur coat, nylon stockings, and a crocodile handbag, I probably wouldn't be sitting here facing you. I gave up all that frippery to visit Europe in 1939 — just as before that I visited Mexico, travelled all over the States, and have been to both Brazil and Argentina."

I was silent. None of those places had ever occurred to me as one I wished to visit. In fact I'd never seen myself as some kind of world traveller. But she wasn't through yet.

"Now take British Columbia, especially the west coast of Vancouver Island. That's about as different as around here as you can imagine. Only the surf is a thing in common. But the snowcapped mountains, the miles of unspoilt beaches and coastline — the sense of unlimited space — well, I'm sure it's beyond your imagination. But it needn't be beyond your pocketbook when you are educated and becoming adult —

provided you haven't already become a little peacock and wasted your money on stupid clothes!"

I perked up. I liked bright colours (especially socks) and didn't like garments that looked flashy and cheap. But a good eye and sense of taste could take care of that — and I was Cornish enough never to indulge in quantity for its own sake. "Tell me about Canada," I said (or something to that effect). And Natalie Guthrie did, from brochure-like descriptions of Banff and Lake Louise to real or invented accounts of small towns and coastal splendours while pointedly ignoring Vancouver and glossing even over her cherished Victoria to concentrate on the Sooke Peninsula and the farmlands of the southern part of Vancouver Island, which she primly informed me was "as large as Wales."

I grew to love Natalie and our long and frequent talks — which were more lectures from her than conversations. I never let on that I owned to a growing interest in my own gender. And when we met up again, some fifteen years later, and I was with my lover, Floyd St. Clair, I think she had difficulty in accepting the implications of his presence. Likewise when she visited us in Vancouver and when we took my mother over to see her again (by which time she was around seventy), she was always polite, often funny, but just that tiny bit held back. Without the specific use of words, which she otherwise used lavishly and with evident relish, she made her negative position patently clear.

Then the experience of meeting people who are intelligent, broad-minded, civilized by travel and encounter, yet who still have difficulty in accepting one's homosexuality has been commonplace in my life. I do not think it will be so, though, for the generations to come. In any case, I am still glad to add the impact and influence of Natalie Guthrie to these pages. After all, some of the sparks she showered on me proved seminal. I owe her for a portion of that immigrant anguish that has fed my creativity as well as my Canadian content as a now rooted British Columbian.

# 4

# CHARLES GOLDBERG

Charles was my buddy at our all-boys school — and I mean buddy and not lover. We met in September 1937 and, as he lived along the Mile End Road, the main thoroughfare out of London passing through the East End, we soon fell into meeting outside his house and walking together the half-mile or so to the Coopers' Company School tucked just off the Mile End Road in the plane tree quiet of Tredegar Square.

We also walked all over Bow, Stepney, and Bethnal Green, investigating street markets and louche little lanes as well as the bustling highways during our lunch hours and again on Wednesdays on those times we played truant from school sports day, which meant the fag of taking the Metropolitan line all the way out to remote Becontree in Essex to play rugger or cricket.

I was soon familiar with mile-long funeral processions with both escorting horses about the hearse and mourners lavish in black crepe as the poor took their dead to the cemetery with an ostentation carefully paid for by years of saving.

I also quickly took in the advertising signs in Hebrew and Yiddish and witnessed numerous fights between those sporting lightning flashes on their armbands (the Fascists) and those with the hammer and sickle (the Commies) and the eventual breakup of the resultant milling mobs by the mounted police.

I also learned shame when I heard my pal referred to by some on the streets as Kike or Yid and saw ubiquitous chalked slogans on fences and railway bridges saying "Down with the Sheenies" or simply "Fuck the Jews."

The harsh truth was there was no shortage in public education during those brief years I daily journeyed to receive my scholastic one — from quiet, middle-class Woodford to the volatile and racially festering East End, where I didn't need the sickness of Hitler's Germany with its swastika'd mobs to observe the sickness of anti-Semitism and see at least the portals of the evil that led a few hundred miles away to the horrors of the Holocaust.

This pattern continued until the summer of 1939, when I headed back once again to Cornwall, and goodness knows what Charley got up to in the heat and stench of that summer in crowded East London.

His father was a bookmaker, and when Charley and I were evacuated with our school to Frome, in Somerset, in 1940, his parents were blown up in the Blitz so that at fourteen he was an orphan. While still in London as day boys our relationship was largely confined to academic camaraderie — we were both smart kids in class — and a certain trading as a result of his being Jewish and I Christian. With the feasts of both faiths we persuaded each other to attend the other's services. He would come and sing in our school choir at Christmas and Easter; I would attend Passover Seder and Yom Kippur and participate in his bar mitzvah and those of his relations and friends. This was not done in any lofty spirit of interfaith respect but out of hard schoolboy bargaining over any perks either of us could muster. We never let the other down over these events and even began to boast about the snippets of the other's religion that we picked up. I would pounce on any Gentile kid who didn't know how many candles there were on a menorah and he could trot off the Nicene Creed as casually as if it were the words of the then-popular song and dance, "The Lambeth Walk."

Removed from London and Cornwall to Somerset, we became much closer — in part through our shared hate of our billeters. His was a middle-aged widow who he swore was sex-starved and who thus constantly sought to seduce him; mine were an aging couple of pious and puritan Baptists who insisted I attend chapel with them and deplored the bad language that was forever on my lips as much as I hated their ruling that the best room in the house was reserved only for Sabbath use, and our breakfasts congealed and grew cold because as we stood shivering each morning in that ice-cold house they insisted on saying a long-winded grace.

Charley enjoyed playing cricket and was in the school's first eleven team. I feared the hard leather ball, besides detesting all sports involving a change of clothes. Yet he was strangely permissive of my total lack of sportsmanship. The permissiveness did not extend to the sunny day I lay next to him on the grass sward as others played in their white shirt and pants in the cricket field and I let my hand stray towards his fly. He gave my groping fingers a hard smack, smiled, and stared at me with his startlingly blue eyes. "No," he said quietly. "I don't do that." And with me he never did.

He really was quite handsome with those blue eyes, wiry athletic body, and head crowned with black curls. He had a snub nose to confound the anti-Semitic cartoonists and was one of the most loyal and generous beings I have ever known.

There was one occurrence that we two shared that neither of us referred to again. We were alone, having a pee side by side in the Victoria Park public toilets one warm summer evening when David Warren, a senior boy from the upper fifth, entered the urinal. Our talk had hitherto been, as usual, of the horrible people we were forced to live with in our billets, but Warren quickly changed all that. "I'm going to toss off in one of the lavs," he announced. "Either want to watch me or help? I'll take the two of you, come to that."

I know a cold thrill swept through me. I knew that if I'd been alone I wouldn't have hesitated. I looked swiftly at Charley. Disdain, revulsion, was all I could see on his face. "Go fuck yourself, Warren," I said in full hypocritical flood. "Pick on your own kind of pervert and for Christ's sake remember where you are! This shitty town hates us evacuees, hates the school — and you want to give 'em ammo with your filthy cock!"

Charley still said nothing, merely grabbed my arm and marched me out into the fresh air. It wasn't until we were there in the reddening sky that we were able to button up our trousers and move as quickly as appearances would allow away from the pointed arches of that squat, red-brick public convenience.

It was in the same week or perhaps a fortnight later that we shared another incident — only this time it was not shame that either felt but fear on my part and embarrassing tears to Charley's eyes as he relived certain memories.

Dusk had fallen and the wartime blackout conditions were in full reign. A number of things followed each other in quick succession. We heard the air-raid siren on the gabled roof of the town hall just before we turned in the direction of Charley's billet, which was quite close to that Victoria Park that again had seen our evening stroll before we settled to our homework in our respective billets (though those subsequent evenings we wordlessly avoided like the plague those Edwardian public conveniences where the sex maniac, Warren, might be hanging around, on the far side of the park).

I think it was Charley, ears tuned from our aircraft recognition class at school, who first heard the throbbing sound of an enemy aircraft, probably Heinkels. At any rate it was he who yelled "Duck" at the whistle of bombs as we hit the turf, followed by the loudest explosion yet to greet my young ears.

That was it. Just one loud crump — then a silence, until, seconds later, flames sprang to life a couple of streets away. From lying there, half under a laurel bush, we heard the sound of either fire engines or ambulances. School training had long taught us that in the event of an air raid we were to stay indoors — and if outside (carrying our gas masks, which we never did) we were to make our way home as soon as we could. This night we disobeyed.

"That sounded like Wellesley Road," I said.

"The Williamsons are billeted there," said Charley. "So is Dennis Lazarus a bit further down."

"Let's go and have a dekko," I said.

Charley pondered that.

"We might be able to help," I added.

Charley reluctantly consented. He was so much more grown up than I was.

When we reached the scene of the air raid "incident," as they were called, there was already a sizeable group of people — air-raid wardens, police, and neighbours — milling around the burning wreckage of what had once been a three-storey Victorian home.

Knowing that, as youngsters, we would be ordered sharply to go home, we hung about the fringes of the small crowd. But not so far that we couldn't see the draped shapes brought out on the stretchers and hear the titter of comment muttered between the onlookers. First it was a small shape that we were told was Clifford Williamson, a red-haired boy who was in our form. He was dead too. But it was after that, when the crowd announced that Cliff's parents had perished as well but had been trapped in the flames, that my friend start to tremble and heave, and then rock in smothered sobs.

Before I could find out what was the matter, Charley turned, said harshly from a suddenly hoarse throat that he had to leave, and disappeared quickly into the dark beyond the flickering twilight of the burning house.

We met as usual the next morning to cycle the mile or more to our school on the outskirts of town, and it was from the fragmented conversation we managed that I was able to piece things together. He had been able, like me, to take the shock and horror of seeing Cliff's still form, arms flopping over the stretcher sides, emerge down the garden steps, but when that had been followed by the blanketed shapes of Carrot Top's parents, Charley's thoughts had gone at once to his own mum and dad and their end in that night of the Blitz just a year before.

He had not been there, had had to rely on second-hand accounts. And ever afterwards had to fight off images that never seemed to go away. I said nothing, couldn't even give him a reassuring jab as we were on our bikes. Then I knew he wouldn't have wanted that. He had never once spoken of their deaths. I had learned about that from Gerry Shapiro, who lived further up the Mile End Road, just past Baum's, the chemists. All Charley had ever done to testify to his loss was to wear that small black velvet patch on the arm of his jacket. And such was commonplace in those days.

Shortly after that our paths separated, even though temporarily. He duly volunteered for the RAF and became a Spitfire pilot while doing his basic air training in Canada (that place again!), whereas I joined the navy and got no further towards the North American continent than a few hundred miles out in the Atlantic Ocean on the deep-sea rescue tug for which we five sailors served as the anti-aircraft defence as we searched for damaged and sinking ships that had fallen out of convoy.

After the war, though, was a different situation. I majored in theology at King's College, London, and then met Floyd, who was doing grad work at "Science Po." While I was tutoring little kids in Paris, Charley got married to the Gentile daughter of a surly Kentish farmer, had two children, and ran a small clothing factory for the garment industry in Soho. We met annually when I returned to England to see my parents in Cornwall and, later, my mother in her widowhood, who had returned to her sylvan suburb of Woodford.

Charley's eyes had retained their bold blueness but his hair had greyed and his skin become lined. Though we were born in the same month, he now looked older than me. He worked so hard in the rag trade, as he invariably called it. Too hard! His wife acted as a buyer for their highly successful firm and sold their unisex bathrobes and the like to classy stores in London and New York. He would entertain me at his club off the Mall and, later, at their comfortable home in an outer suburb in Hertfordshire.

It was at the latter venue that a strange incident took place — an event that subtly altered our relationship but not the depth of our affection, which had become real and deep over the years. The evening began ordinarily enough. We shared drinks while Susan prepared dinner. The teenage son and daughter were out of the house. Suddenly Charley got up from his sherry, and as he headed out of the room he muttered, "There's something I want to show you."

It was right after that his wife put her head around the kitchen door. "Where's Charley gone?"

"To fetch something he thinks I should see."

Her body followed her head into the room. "Oh, yes. Those papers. They must be getting musty after all these years. He started collecting them when he was in love with you. Where was that? Somerset, wasn't it, where you two were schoolkids together?"

I had no possible words at hand with which to reply. Fortunately Charley returned at that moment, clutching a green Harrods shopping bag from which peeped a whole sheaf of papers.

"There they are," he said, his usually quiet voice rather vibrant in triumph. "Every single one of them!"

"Of what?" My own voice was very faint so that we vocally constituted a reversal to our normal roles.

"Every English composition you wrote for Mr. Howes and Mr. Coles. The one you did for your brother and got the cane from Mr. Howes for being too smart. And the essays you did on wild animals as pets you wrote for Mr. Williams in biology and also the ones you wrote for the *Cooperian*." As he spoke he was carefully taking them out of the shopping bag and laying them before me on the coffee table.

I remembered getting the cane (three strokes on the bum) for writing for my brother, Brian, a first-person imaginary trip up the Orinoco, which I overdid by killing off the narrator when he and his friends fell out of the boat and were all devoured by piranhas. But there my recollection ground to a halt.

Charley, on the other hand, had been the indefatigable historian of the literary endeavours of David Arthur Watmough when at the Coopers' Company School. He drew sheet after sheet of exercise book paper filled with my atrocious scrawl and laid them before me — startling ghosts of an era utterly buried under subsequent years of wholly other experience. As I looked I of course remembered but it could as easily have been of another person as it indeed was of another place and time.

As I read — no, scanned — I was deeply aware of Charley watching me, a smile on his lips and his eyes less frosty and remote than usual as he proudly regarded me. I finally put the last page down atop the now considerable pile. He was addressing me: "They're all there, I think. You see, David Arthur" — that was what he and he alone had always called me at relaxed moments — "I just knew you were going to be a famous writer ..."

"Well, I'm certainly not that," I interjected. "One book on the French Church and a couple of volumes of short stories don't add up to 'famous.'"

"Will be famous," he added. "No doubt in my book, and I was determined to be the keeper of, what do they call it? Your *juvenilia*. All that should end up in the British Museum, you know."

"Bullshit," I said.

He started to put the schoolboy scribblings back into the Harrods bag. "In that case I shall hold on to these until your decease. You're not to be trusted with them with that attitude!" And he took them and presumably replaced them whence he'd found them.

Poor Charley! He became deceased long before me, I swear from overwork at that bloody garment factory and all the worries of the world that he seemed to attract. Not having anything tangible of him and our friendship of nigh forty years, these memories I have set down become the cherished link that will be unbroken in the time I have left, sadly bereft of the benison of seeing him again.

# 5

# Three Major Incidents Between Westminster and the Strand

It didn't happen every day, but where except London in the England of 1945–50 was I likely to bump into a prime minister, a world-famous playwright, and the wife of an American president, who was a remarkable woman in her own right?

All three of these people I encountered on my daily early morning walk, which took me from Vincent Square in Westminster where I lived in the King's College Theological Hostel, across Victoria Street, down the narrow lane of Petit France and the London Transport Building with its flanking Epstein sculptures, along Birdcage Walk bordering the water birds and bulbs in springtime of St. James's Park, past the brick-walled back gardens of 10 Downing Street, along the Embankment, and finally down the Strand to Somerset House and, very next door, the arched entrance to King's College and the oldest college of the University of London to Somerset House — both buildings of Portland stone and both overlooking the Embankment and the curving Thames.

I shall start with the woman, as she represented my first physical brush with the famous. I refer to Eleanor Roosevelt, wife of the American president, who was present in London in the fall of 1945 as the United States representative at the second meeting ever (after the inaugural in San Francisco) of the United Nations. I am hardly claiming Eleanor Roosevelt as a friend, or even as a close acquaintance, as our encounter lasted but a matter of minutes. Even so my physical collision, followed by instant recognition from the newspapers, with this portly American first lady on the steps of Westminster Hall on Parliament Square had a profound effect on me.

One thing it certainly did change was a teenage undergraduate's attitude towards the famous forevermore. I learned with the speed of a rifle bullet, not only that they were actually human, but that they could be warm and motherly — well, at least auntlike.

This is what happened. As usual I was late for classes and was cantering along the streets outlined above, oblivious of little else but the fact that I could ill afford to miss Dr. Eric Jay's lecture on *The Summa Theologica* of Aquinas. We were reading the texts in Latin — a language at which I was even less competent than Samuel Johnson purported Shakespeare to be, and with a Greek likewise more paltry than the Bard's!

Latin, though I prayed in it, I never liked, whereas my crumbs of Greek I learned to love. In fact my total academic scholarship might be summed up as something more loved than learned. The truth is I was a lousy student.

Perhaps I was reflecting dolefully on that very fact when I knocked down the U.S. delegate to the UN. She was easing her not inconsiderable figure up the same broad step that I was traversing at breakneck speed as part of my shortcut across Parliament Square. I may have imagined the faint smell of lavender or some other scent; what I did not imagine was the softness of her as we fell in a heap on the hard stone.

In those days I'd never heard of security guards, the FBI, and that stuff, but in any event, none such materialized. A little later a British bobby started to amble in our direction, but by that time we were sitting, chatting, and preparing to stand up again. I say chatting but really it was a Q & A routine directed by Mrs. Roosevelt. She just enveloped my spluttered apologies and efforts at self-deprecation and asked me instead who I was and what I did. I later came to realize there was an authority to her manner that bespoke an aristocracy existing on the other side of the Atlantic and I found that confirmed by personal experience a few years hence. But there was nothing harsh or forbidding about her questions. They were more like those of an anxious aunt concerned to reassure and allay all fears.

While she was about to participate in debates that would set the world aright and deal with matters that still affect our globe today, she asked me where my parents lived — the Cornish bit seemed to intrigue her — and what I intended to do after graduation. I did strive for a little wit by suggesting that there might be no graduation if I missed my Latin class on Thomas Aquinas, and I shall never know whether the gigantic whoop it elicited from her was a genuine response to my clumsy humour or yet another effort to calm me and help me collect my senses. By the time the cop arrived and she began work on calming and reassuring him, I was making my goodbyes, expressing my good wishes to her husband (he happened to be a hero of mine), and hoping that she would enjoy her time in the British Isles. Her last words to me, I think, were "Now do well in your studies, young man."

I stopped at the bottom of the flight of steps to see her broad and suited figure go inside.

Another incident, although far less dramatic and certainly not life-informing, was the frequency that we (the students often walked in pairs from Vincent Square, with its spacious green space —the playing fields of Westminster School — to College) encountered the prime minister of those postwar years, Clement Atlee.

Short, dapper — he still stiffly bore the rank of major from his earlier army career. He, too, was devoid of a sizeable bodyguard. Presumably it was a plainclothes policeman that accompanied him but I don't remember Britain's leading statesman with any other protection. It seemed that he took his early morning "constitutional" in the vicinity of St. James's Park at the same time we headed east for classes, preceded by chapel if it were a major feast day.

There was always a smile for us as we greeted him and always a reply to our salutations.

"Good morning, sir!"

"Good morning... Good morning!"

Small beer maybe. But it reaffirmed that even then, at the twilight of the British Empire, a degree of simple humanity remained in that particular human pyramid between the man at the top and we lesser mortals.

Of course the politically minded might say that, after all, he headed the Labour Party and that socialists were duty-bound to demonstrate such camaraderie. But it has been my experience that politicians and statesmen in democracies are not always in accordance with the ideas of equality and mutual respect that are constantly thrown about. In my third year I became local president of what was then unfortunately known by the initials FUCA: the Federation of University Conservative Associations. Labour had been in power for three years; we young Tories were the rebels. Indeed, I wouldn't be surprised that the same young men and women would have been Labour or at least Liberal had the Conservatives been in power. Such is mutinous youth.

During that brief period I welcomed a number of MPs of all parties and none to address us at King's. They included the Australian Brendan Bracken, a stalwart Winston Churchill supporter and loudmouth, the Labour MP Tom Driberg — an easy recruit for organizations of any political persuasion if young male students were involved in running them — and Douglas Jay, who became economic secretary to the treasury under Cripps and whom I found the nicest of the lot. He actually asked students what they were studying and, unlike the rest, didn't speak exclusively of himself and his virtues. So many politicians are as self-absorbed as actors — only without the blessed limitation of the theatre.

An altogether different encounter, though like those with the PM it was one that occurred on a regular basis through the successive university terms, was that with the famous elderly playwright George Bernard Shaw. Unlike the brief utterances of the ex-major prime minister, those of G.B.S. were fluty high and more sustained. There were still traces of his Irish heritage in his voice, but an out and out brogue it was not. We generally exchanged salutations, but he would sometimes observe that it was a day ripe for mischief or caution that we weren't to pick all the flowers there in the beds in order to bribe the teacher.

These encounters took place in the Embankment Gardens, and I believe he lived in an apartment there for at least that part of the year he wasn't in Ayot St. Lawrence in Hertfordshire. He was not only eminently recognizable but strongly resembled my bearded Great-Uncle Robert in Cornwall, who preceded my parents by a generation as resident of the dower house opposite Mr. Lightfoot's "bewitched" cottage.

Uncle Robert always lurked about his garden gate on clement days, wearing a straw panama and often a white suit. He looked very Edwardian. G.B.S. was never without a hat above his white beard, and I have a strong suspicion that his perambulations around his section of the Embankment Gardens was also motivated by the hope of casual and limited encounter with the likes of us early in the morning.

There were other reasons for my spirits rising on the days we encountered this man than for the fact he was famous. I knew he was very ancient and that alone intrigued me, as I have always been attracted by the very elderly of our species and always sought to learn from those of them still possessed of their faculties as G.B.S. obviously was. The learning from him, though, was oblique to say the least — namely a progressive familiarity with his plays, much stimulated by these morning sightings.

But the author of those works such as *Saint Joan*, *Caesar and Cleopatra*, *Man and Superman*, *The Doctor's Dilemma*, and *Major Barbara*, which are still being performed a century later, and who himself was born in 1856, has played a strange role in my life as a conduit of history.

I still have in my possession a volume titled *G.B.S. 90*, which was a Festschrift for his ninetieth birthday in 1946. It is personally inscribed to me on my own twentieth birthday as follows: "To The Stripling from the Sage ... David — minium decadit, Ambrose." That "Ambrose" was the Reverend Ambrose Weekes, Chaplain, RN, who found an unhappy, rudderless me as an ordinary seaman, renewed my self-respect, introduced me to the College of the Sea that sent textbooks and other volumes to those wishing to feed their minds, and sparked my ambition to attend university when I was discharged.

All in all, a pretty important factor in my life. And although I saw little of the reverend when the war was over and he became a continental chaplain and subsequently the bishop of Gibraltar he indubitably helped course my future. But the fact of G.B.S. and the gift from Ambrose Weekes was yet further compounded as a conduit of history for me. In the pages of the Shaw volume I discover I have long ago inserted a slip of paper. On it in bold and large longhand is inscribed the message, "I've sent the Carriage — Come quick, & the Coachman will pick me up! Nell."

I have no idea who "Nell" is, though I recall finding the note in a first edition of Tennyson's *In Memoriam* given to me in Paris by a lady as old as Shaw and whose father was a physician with his surgery on the Champs Élysées in the nineteenth century. In those days from the Etoile to the Rond Point was all private residences and the physician was forbidden to place a brass plate bearing his name and profession outside his apartment. My friend furnished this information when, with a youthful sigh in 1950, I exclaimed how the Champs Élysées was becoming ruined commercially and she felt it necessary to tell me how she had felt similar sentiments in 1900, and that such reactions were often very relative. Then Gertrude Brandreth (née Reynaud) was a wise woman, perhaps as wise as George Bernard Shaw.

# 6

# ERIC SYMES ABBOTT

In the heady, late-adolescent days in the aftermath of the Second World War (when I strove to resurrect the unsullied youth who had, centuries earlier, dreamily wandered the lonely lanes of Cornwall before first embracing the dirt of war and the hammock-ubiquity of other sexually aroused sailors), I came close for the one and only time in my life to worshipping another human being.

The man in question was a one-time canon of Lincoln Cathedral who became eventually the dean of Westminster Abbey with a knighthood and honorary doctorate. When I first encountered him (through the aegis of Ambrose Weekes, my naval chaplain, who had been a student of his at Lincoln), he was an inspired spiritual director in his late thirties who exuded a spiritual innocence (that was nothing to do with ignorance), exemplified the cultural refinements of Jesus College, Cambridge, and possessed the most beautiful spoken voice I'd ever heard.

In other words he reflected the very opposite of the traits I felt begrimed me. I was a nineteen-year-old student already with an impressive sexual track record. Eric Abbott — even his surname evoked ecclesiastical matters!

I was essentially uneducated; prone to mispronouncing foreign names that I loved to utter; generally unlettered; altogether ignorant of the arts; and knowing really nowhere but farms and dung-flecked lanes, alternating with a quiet suburban street brimming with social pretension, and subsequently the confining, uncouth life on a small ship afloat on the cold grey waters of the North Atlantic.

All that before I was nineteen, when I climbed the fanned steps of King's College Hostel in Vincent Square and would remain, with the warden as the primary influence on my person, for the next four highly informing years.

Eric, whom I soon learned was from Nottingham (a town I visualized as the home of dainty lace and the manly site of Player's cigarettes), not only still carried the social poise of his pre-war Cambridge with him, but knew intimately, as an ardent convert Londoner, this big, dirty, and bomb-battered city where we both now dwelt in our separate stations as student and warden of King's College Theological Hostel facing Westminster School's tree-bordered playing fields in Vincent Square.

I had broken schoolboy French; he could turn swiftly and deftly from Greek to Latin. I knew the bands of Henry Hall, Joe Loss, Jack Payne, and Ambrose. He played records of Schubert and Schumann, of Brahms and Beethoven, in his cream-carpeted drawing room with its chintz sofas and armchairs and gilt-framed Johann Adam Ackermann prints lining the walls.

He spoke an English that was laced with classical and biblical allusion and easily avoided both the burr of provincialism and the plumminess of class affectation. My time was cut out to avoid using such Cornishisms as "well, I do reckon" and terms like "maze" for "stupid" and "wishy" for "bad weather" that neither my fellow students nor my professors at King's College had ever heard of!

From my first day in Eric's world I set out to be a snob and strove to be a pedant. He never betrayed either affliction. (Well, that is almost true.) He did tell me once that a certain plebeian but socially ambitious student whom we both knew was "no advertisement for the college, boy." This was by the time I had given up on the arcane escalator of English snobbery as "unnecessary for us Celts" and acquired a decent confidence in the arts (at Eric's inspiration), which has been an assuagement of the years and indeed determined that I eventually become a practitioner of literature.

But I stray too far ahead. In the middle 1940s, when this man was the centre of my social and academic universe, my rarely inactive homosexuality was not a subject we alluded to in any open way. He knew I was queer, of course. For I had arrived at the college as a naval discharge for "importuning and soliciting" and questions of my eventual ordination were to be held in abeyance until this flaw of character and sin of practice had either been expunged or sublimated. But I perceived him to be *sympathique* — indeed, he actively encouraged me in a hothouse affair with a fellow student at the hostel. John, who was a year younger, had missed war service and had emerged from a minor English public school a total snob, mildly anti-Semitic, and, inconsistently, a good if minor pianist who had seen the tutelage of Clifford Curzon.

For three years I slept with him regularly both in one of our neighbouring rooms and during vacations at my house or his. And Eric was fully cognizant of the fact. One small cameo involves him looking at his watch below the sleeve of the simple sarum cassock he invariably wore in the warden's house as we finished listening to Schubert's *Octet in F Major* and announcing, "Well, boy, time for bed. I'm sure John is awaiting you."

Yet the fact remains that while he would often hug my shoulders, squeeze my hand, favour me generally above the hundred or so other student residents between the fall of 1945 and the summer of 1949, there was never a hint of sex between us and never overt encouragement or recognition of the louche adventures that my promiscuity created — even though it brought me back to Vincent Square in the small hours and the dean of King's College (his title away from the hostel) himself had to unlock the door and let me in.

But my fascination with Eric, the power and influence he has had permanently upon me in countless ways, cannot, I think, be reduced to opposite degrees of cultural and spiritual poverty at a specific period in his life and mine.

With twenty-twenty hindsight and with him dead and me in my eighties, I can say that our gay mutuality was definitely an element, as was the fact that he was so ineluctably successful in that ecclesiastical-qua-academic world he had elected to dwell in from his dean of King's College, London, days when he became also a royal chaplain to King George VI, then warden of Keble College, Oxford, before attaining the summit of the Westminster deanery (he had steadfastly refused all bishoprics from the Prime Minister's Office).

Whereas on the other hand by my third decade I had confronted failure at virtually every turn. Since age eleven I had failed every important exam I had undertaken, seen arrest and imprisonment as a pervert, and been a laughingstock sailor whose ineptitude may well have delayed the successful conclusion of the war by a microsecond.

Until I met Eric and spent those four years under his tutelage, I was an unhappy and uncertain figure who was given to acute depression and faced the unknown future with horror. Perhaps, then, the attraction of opposites?

What I think was the most precious benison I received from the man of whom I write here was the gift of faith: his nourishing faith in me over those early years that in conjunction with the ensuing vital and reassuring confidence in my creativity bestowed by my lifetime lover, Floyd, flowered finally as faith in myself.

In 1951, in contributing a preface to my very first book, A *Church Renascent: A Study in Modern French Catholicism*, he wrote, "this book is the work and offering of a young man [I was then twenty-five] with a temperament and a spirituality closely akin to our brothers in France, 'sympathique' in a special degree, not merely to what is being done there but to the spirit in which it is being done."

I personally see that as a typically "Abbottian" coded message that addresses not so much my Gallican personality as my gay one.

Some twenty years later, when I was visiting him from Vancouver and we were walking on the roof of Westminster Abbey, of which world-famous shrine he had now become dean, he told me that he had always believed in me — even though he had to preside painfully over my failure to gain a degree — and as we wandered along the ancient leads overlooking the Houses of Parliament, he added that his faith in my talents had now been vindicated.

Apart from the fact that his praise was usually couched in rather excessive terms, I detected a new note this time. It was that of finality. My sense was — is — that he was telling me that his mission over me was now discharged and at that very moment I had the feeling we would never meet again. And that was so. We exchanged Christmas cards and the occasional letter but that was all. He suffered a second, perhaps third, heart attack and duly retired from the abbey and public life.

Later I heard that he had a boyfriend tucked away in the country and that had been the case for many covert years. There were also subsequent rumours that someone would be writing his biography. But that has not come to pass. I doubt whether it ever will, as personalities of major ecclesiastical figures in the Church of England no longer count for much. And there is the further bleak truth that there are progressively fewer of us left who were touched and blessed by him. (And I am not so vain as to believe his ministry to young men was not a large-scale undertaking over the years.)

But historical fashions — like literary ones — mean little to me, and I have been determined to affirm his *sui generis* influence on my life ever since I was an emotionally ragged teenager and he so rewardingly entered it to give me an education as rich and informing as that of any institution, sacred or secular.

# 7
# FATHER HENRY RENAUD
# TURNER BRANDRETH, OGS

The above title is precisely how he would have wanted to be listed. It proclaimed his priesthood, reflected his aristocratic background, and concealed his lack of an academic degree. This is the person of all those evoked in these memoirs that I most regret being dead. I would have liked to publicly attest his importance in our lives and the extraordinary generosity he revealed to determine that Floyd and I start our over fifty years' passage together — all while he could read it. It is also the last priestly presence I have to record as causing a major dent in the persona of David Watmough.

Henry was in many senses (though he took enormous pains to conceal it) a modest and uncertain man. He was convinced he was ugly and preferred his gay sex clandestine and preferably in the dark. The fact that a more parentally beloved and beautiful brother predeceased him in a tragic air accident when he was a yet a young man did not increase his self-esteem or confidence.

When I first met him, in Paris in 1947, he was a slim, prematurely bald Anglican priest who had just become the incumbent of St. George's Church in the French capital. I was a twenty-one-year-old student erotically pursuing my companion, a fellow undergraduate of King's College, London, and we were en route to the French Alps on what was our first trip to the war-ravaged Continent.

At that time neither of Henry's parents were there, but two years later, when I stayed in the presbytery while writing my book on the priest-worker movement in the French church, both Gertrude and "Jake" were present. The former was a tall, elderly woman of regal composure and demeanour whose maiden name was Renaud; she was the daughter of a Parisian doctor who as a girl in the nineteenth century lived on the Champs Élysées between the Arc de Triomphe and the Seine when that area was wholly residential.

However, she was also first cousin to her husband, who never recovered from being an infantry officer on the Western Front and who subsequently became a drunk with a penchant for robbing the Peter's Pence boxes in the church to sustain his habit of consuming cheap red wine whilst his son's guest in France.

Gertrude described for me later, when we had become friends and she had met my mother and my aunt, that as a girl she had often visited her Brandreth cousins at stately Houghton Hall in Huntingdonshire, and after dinner each night, when the last male had slid drunk under the table, her mother-in-law would gesture to her and any other ladies present to rise as she suggested so that they might now gravitate to the drawing room for coffee. It sounded Hogarthian to me – then there was something about "Jake" and even Henry at times that was entirely redolent of the eighteenth century.

It was soon apparent that vast fortunes had been drunk or gambled away over a century or three. Henry always claimed proudly that one of his Devonian ancestors had been hanged as a highwayman and – with equal relish – that his Aunt Minnie was renowned in Bournemouth as a scavenger of dustbins and other sources for discarded treasures. Although in her case her lowly pursuit was cited as the result of eccentricity rather than poverty.

In her last years Gertrude Brandreth became a close friend of my mother and her close friend, my honorary "Aunt" Elsie, who had visited her in Paris when I was living there. She enjoyed their company and perhaps there was a secret bond with my mother in the cost of sharing gay sons. In any case, she always seemed at her happiest in their company.

Henry was a complicated person, and his many sides were usually known only to those who shared such facets. He was, for instance, a good, if minor, poet – with works published by the Indian poet Tambimuttu in his *Poetry London* magazine during and immediately after the Second World War. A poem, "The Tulip," dedicated to me, demonstrated both his sensuous strengths and intellectual limitations as a poet issuing from his solipsistic horizons. His eager pursuit of arcane fact and byways of ecclesiastical history resulted in several published books and articles from his ancient typewriter, on which he was surprisingly proficient. He had an almost Buddhist reverence for animal life and was equally devoted to his Parisian cat, Bast, and a rat that inhabited the dark corridors and stairways of le *presbytère* that he named Horace. He was often drunk and even more frequently choleric. He was politically to the right of Attila the Hun yet claimed friends of many nationalities. He would have been sexually promiscuous if chance had better offered. Yet I do believe he took his life as a member of the Cambridge-based Oratory of the Good Shepherd very seriously and had a real affection for his brethren. No one who knew him would ever have described him as consistent.

Henry's impact on me was more on my life than on my person. Temperamentally we were poles apart, and if he were not in love with me, the lion's share of our time together — which covered nearly two years in Paris — would have surely been spent in altercation. But it was under his aegis and through his generosity that on a certain Wednesday in late September 1951 I met Floyd St. Clair under his roof, fell in love with him, and thus changed radically the geographical contours of my life.

It is a story I have often told but — not least for the romantically inclined — I will adumbrate it once more. It was the custom at St. George's Anglican Church in Paris, of which Father Henry Brandreth was the chaplain, to devote Wednesday evenings to visiting English-speaking students of any or no denomination, offering them sherry, wine, or coffee and social time with each other and the resident priest in his book-lined study. On that particular evening pertinent to this account, I absented myself from the event, as I was suffering from a toothache. However, another young resident of the *presbytère*, Dr. Keith Maillard, came bounding up the steep and narrow staircase to my room, which led out onto the lead roofs of the rue Auguste Vacquerie, and insisted I come down to "Father's study," as a group of American students had arrived and he, Keith, was convinced that one of them spelled me. After some protestation I descended three floors and entered the room from which came the noisy chorus of several young people and, even louder, the voice of their host. I scanned the score or so faces, both boys and girls, seated mainly cross-legged on the carpet, alighted on that of Floyd, tall, blond, and crew-cut, and then and there fell in love.

I squeezed myself down next to him and his companion, a fellow grad student at the Sorbonne and also from Stanford University in California. There was not much chance of personal conversation in those circumstances — Henry invariably dominated such assemblies — but I did manage to ask him whether he would be attending Mass the following Sunday, which would be a major event as it was the Feast of St. Michael and all the Angels — in other words, Michaelmas Day. For the record I couldn't have cared less whether it was Mass Murderer's Day — my sole motive was to see this captivating son of California again.

We did. And from then on I journeyed frequently to the apartment that he and Frank Rudman shared on the avenue Niel in the adjacent *arrondissement*. I told Henry of all this, omitting only the carnal details — not out of delicacy towards his own feelings as my would-be-but-forever-frustrated lover but from my own deep-rooted prudery.

Then came the surprise. We were approaching the weekend of November 11, which was Armistice Day in France, and a solemn holiday when a nation recalled the millions of its wartime dead. Henry suddenly said one evening when we were having too many cocktails at the bar belonging to the retired world champion boxer Georges Carpentier, hard by the Champs Élysées, that it was time Floyd and I took time out to go away for a couple of days and see whether we were really of significance to each other. Not only that, he was prepared to pay for a short train trip and hotel accommodation at the other end.

He was as good as his then-slurred word, and the following weekend, when it rained unceasingly, Floyd and I found ourselves in a small hostelry in the cathedral city of Senlis, just north of Paris. My memories are now as blurred as the view from our rain-splashed bedroom window, but I do recall two rare departures from what we afterwards referred to as our nuptial bed. One was to brave the wet and pick glistening blackberries from huge bramble piles edging a sodden field; the other was to attend at the Solemn Requiem Mass for Armistice Day in the cathedral. The sermon was preached by the elderly bishop, who spent most of his time regaling the congregation of his grim years as an army chaplain during the First World War and reminding us of the perpetrated horrors of the Hun and the continuing threat of barbarianism from the east towards the civilized and cultural flowers of La Belle France.

We were still seeing Henry years later, when we returned on vacation from the United States and subsequently Canada. And he was always keen to see us, first in Paris and subsequently in London, where he worked as an ecumenical consultant to Michael Ramsay, archbishop of Canterbury at Lambeth Palace. But there was something missing. Henry never found another me to love until it hurt, but his heart did heal. He moved on and Floyd and I became merely part of the panoply of his past life.

# 8
# WYSTAN HUGH AUDEN

It began with an exchange of correspondence, between Holy Cross Monastery on the west bank of the Hudson River at West Park, just north of Poughkeepsie, and the Island of Ischia, off the coast of Italy. The note on the picture postcard was in the neat small hand of W.H. Auden, in answer to my inquiry and the enclosure of my poems, informing me that he and Chester Kallman would be back in New York City later that month and that he would duly be getting in touch with me from their apartment on St. Mark's Place.

He was as good as his word — Auden always was — and thus I found myself staring up at a rather shabby apartment from the curb opposite where a few dry leaves rustled about my feet on a Saturday afternoon in the fall of 1954. I should describe my state of mind at that moment, as I am sure it coloured my subsequent reactions after that paint-peeling front door opened and a thickset man in felt bedroom slippers peered down at me with an expansive smile and greeted me in a strong British accent with all the vowels rigorously flattened for transatlantic consumption.

It took me a little while to grasp that he wasn't being affected or deliberately idiosyncratic but merely acting out what I eventually perceived was just Audenesque logic. He was British-born and therefore spoke accordingly. But he had lived in the United States for thirteen years and so dutifully reflected that fact by making *can't* rhyme with *cant*.

After the hybrid accent the next major impact on me was via my nose rather than my ears. The distinctly untidy and rather dimly lit apartment into which he ushered me smelled distinctly of cat. And I am not referring to the fur or even breath of the loud-mouthed Siamese that glided in every direction. I mean the contents of a cat box — which I eventually located in the cramped and crowded lavatory, which again suggested that neither occupant was an ardent or particularly hygienic housekeeper.

The notion of a spotless habitation (and remember I had just come from a monastery cell that morning) was not furthered by the fact that they were both heavy smokers. There were brimming ashtrays everywhere and lots of ashes scattered over the dining table, across the worn carpet, and on chair arms that had never reached any kind of receptacle.

In short, the place was a mess, but the stink was pungent and overwhelmingly pervasive. Neither of them seemed aware of it, however, and when I eventually plucked up enough courage to make a pertinent comment to my host, Wystan remarked casually that he thought one of the cats (so there must have been two) had missed the cat box in the john and used the carpet instead.

I murmured something about the cat pee having something in common with cigarette ash but he was having none of that. "No such thing," he said crisply, using his schoolmaster manner with which I was to become subsequently very familiar. "In fact what is stinking is cat shit not pee. Chester, I wrote 'cat litter' down on your shopping list and for the second time you didn't bring it. That shitty stuff has been in there for nearly a month. No wonder it stinks to high heaven and it is upsetting Mr. Watmough. He has the most delicate nostrils, coming from a monastery."

Up to that moment he had been calling me "David," so I knew I was being reproved. My next words did not help matters. "I've just run out of cigarettes. Do you think I could borrow one of yours until I can slip out and get some?"

He faced me from the other end of the substantial dining table where he was prone to preside for most of the time. "In the first instance, young man, cigarettes are not borrowed, as when smoked they are incapable of being returned. In the second, in this household where we are all smokers, it is incumbent upon each to supply his own." He added something about that being the only practical method of good housekeeping. But as I looked about me I had to forcibly restrain myself from making some wisecrack.

Then, in an odd way, this otherwise formidable man who brimmed with erudition and genuine interest in me and, for that matter, my family back in Cornwall, was strangely vulnerable. Though I am not sure he was always aware of the fact.

Another aspect of his vulnerability wasn't manifest until much later that evening. First was the departure of Chester to go cruising the naval dockyards in Brooklyn. The second was when the poet attempted unsuccessfully — and only the once — to have sex with me in the big and rumpled bed (God knows when it was last properly made!) that we duly shared, when he shyly though mutely revealed that he was the possessor of a truly tiny, uncircumcised penis.

I don't wish to dwell unduly on such anatomical details but I am convinced that his genital deficiency (or rather his sense of such) was a profoundly informing constituent to Wystan's psychological and emotional makeup. In like vein, the fact that his Jewish lover, Chester, had a large and cut member was a sturdy anchor to the poet's romantic affections.

But that is speculation. What I am concerned to do here is to offer the reader possible material that he or she will not have encountered elsewhere. So let me revert to details and to that very first weekend.

I had not been in the apartment for half an hour before he was questioning me quite vigorously about my father, the state of his health, and his attitudes to life in postwar Britain. It was not that he ignored my mother and her well-being, but then and on virtually every occasion I subsequently stayed over the weekend with them on the Lower East Side, he made it a prominent routine to inquire first of my father and to ask whether I had heard from him since my last visit to New York City. After a month or so I remembered to take letters from Dad with me from the monastery and to read them aloud to Wystan.

The pattern lasted a year until, in fact, I returned to England when my father suffered a heart attack on St. Enodoc golf course near his ancestral home in North Cornwall. I never saw Wystan Auden again, although we continued to correspond intermittently — especially when he and his entourage were in Ischia and subsequently residing in Upper Austria.

Another factor that sticks in my mind from that fairly intense year when I spent so many weekends at St. Mark's Place was our shared interest in music, especially opera. He had recently purchased two LP albums of works by Vincenzo Bellini: *Norma* and *I Puritani* – both with Maria Callas and on Angel recordings.

I sensed that he was a recent convert to both the composer and the soprano. In any case, he played the records at full blast and with loud comments of boyish enthusiasm at frequent intervals. For this musical session we sat again at the dining table with the cats still much in evidence both olfactorily and in their physical agility when they jumped on us, the table, and occasionally on the record player itself. These feline interruptions in no way fazed my host, who was patently transported by Bellini's music and the dramatic interpretation of Callas.

I don't think we ever had another day or evening together when opera wasn't discussed – though sometimes it was little more than mere gossip about Igor Stravinsky, his bitchy amanuensis Robert Craft, and the genesis and initial production of *The Rake's Progress*, for which Auden had contributed the libretto.

It was in that context he mentioned both Benjamin Britten and his fellow expatriate to the United States, Christopher Isherwood, who had taken up permanent residence on the West Coast. For neither of these two native Englishmen did the poet evince an excess of generosity. But his reservations were considerably more over the composer than the novelist.

I must stress here that over neither was Auden as scratchy or as unpleasantly vituperative as I have heard others be. And behind his strictures (and he was inclined to be schoolmarm critical of nearly everybody at some stage or the other) there was usually a moral charge in his mind.

For instance, I received the impression that he was irritated because Britten returned to England during the war. And that he was rather cross with Isherwood for deserting New York for Los Angeles.

I must now come to the prime reason I made the acquaintance of this truly great man and acknowledge my abiding debt to him. It was the Christian religion in its Anglican/Episcopalian format that really enabled me to meet Auden in the first place and, however ironic it may sound in the context of what I have already written, was a primary constituent of our relationship as it continued throughout that and the subsequent year.

By the second Sunday of our acquaintanceship I had accompanied a bedroom-slippered Auden to Mass at the local St. Mark's Church and embarrassedly left with him when, as the priest mounted the pulpit after Holy Communion to deliver the sermon, I was told in a loud stage whisper that the man was a poorer preacher than he certainly was and I most likely was — and noisily got up from knees to go.

Shortly after that I was accompanying Wystan to various Christian meetings on weekday evenings, such as those of the "Nails Movement," which celebrated the Crucifixion and Suffering of the atoning Saviour. If memory serves, these were usually held in rather plush Upper East Side apartments and it was here that I met such Christian intellectual luminaries as Auden's Protestant friends, the Niehburs; the dynamic founder of the *Catholic Worker*, Dorothy Day; and a sprinkling of Jesuits, Dominicans, and other ecumenically minded theologians for whom Wystan entertained a warm respect and often glowing affection. On these occasions the poet was patently very relaxed and quite at home — even though pulling me by the hand behind him and introducing me as his young friend from Holy Cross Monastery on the Hudson.

Another sharply etched memory encompasses what — not for the first or last time in my life — proved to be a benison although at first perceived in purely negative terms. I am referring to Auden's reaction to my poetry.

With the temerity of the young I had sent him a sheaf of work I had recently published in *Holy Cross Magazine* — which I was fortuitously co-editing at the time as part of my general and somewhat vague employment at the monastery.

Now there are as many myths about famous homos flattering comely young unknown gays as there are about nymphets, movie directors, and casting couches. In the case of W.H. Auden I can state unequivocally that his literary judgments were in no way informed by the prospect of sex in bed with this particular supplicant.

He may have eyed me appreciatively that first time I entered his home, but I had barely sat down before he roundly informed me that after reading my verses he was advising me never to write another word of purported verse, religiously inspired (as most of mine was) or otherwise.

I assiduously followed his advice, until I became eighty and started my sonnets sequence, and never felt cause to be less than utterly grateful for the pains he took to shatter my youthful illusions. I can still recall poetry from that time — and shudder to think of it in print. My only regret has been my inability to be as trenchantly honest about the gifts of others I have met when roles have been somewhat reversed from those I knew with that craggy-faced, crumpled curmudgeon whom I consider the finest poet in our language since his co-religionist, T.S. Eliot.

There is a postscript to this brief evocation of the only man I have ever encountered whom I quite unselfconsciously refer to as great and whose painfully wrought and cultivated religious faith is something I have never ceased wishing, and hopefully striving, to emulate. It is a rather sad if instructive postscript.

A few years later, on a sustained visit to England and a temporary appointment as a radio producer with the BBC, I encountered a likeable— no, loveable —"literary" duffer named Derek Patmore.

One ill-omened evening I told Derek of meeting Auden in New York and how much the poet meant to me and that one day I would like to publicly witness to the fact in print. What I didn't know then but was shortly to be made only too cognizant of was that Derek was an ineluctable and incessant gossip and tittle-tattle.

It was only when my last two letters to Auden received no reply that I began slowly to learn what had happened. Derek had told Wystan that I was about to write an all-revealing account of my youthful gay life in New York and elsewhere and that Auden would feature largely in such an account. In vain did I write to reassure him that such was not the case and that I had no intention of ever writing my memoirs or of being indiscreet over the private lives of friends. It was only many years later, when in retrospect I learned the poet was dying, that he wrote to the Canadian High Commissioner in London expressing regret at his inability to attend a forthcoming reading I was giving at Canada House and making some nice noises on my behalf. I took that to mean I was finally forgiven and was once again trusted.

# 9
# GITTA SERENY

y second visit and first sustained contact with New York City
was something of a boomerang affair. I had just rejoined Floyd
in his native California (after his return from Paris and my subsequent saving of enough pennies to cross the Atlantic), when the Korean
War took him — not to Asia but back to France — to Orleans as a French
translator for the U.S. Army.

Left high and dry at Stanford, where I'd gone to be with him and
work at the library during his grad work for a PhD, I ached to be closer
than a continent and an ocean, so I took the *California Zephyr* train to Chicago and the *Twentieth Century Limited* from there to New York, where a
job had been arranged for me from within the Episcopal church network
with the press of an upstate monastery.

I met Gitta Sereny and her husband, Don Honeyman, a fashion photographer with *Vogue*, during that year I was spending weekdays at Holy Cross
Monastery at West Park, on the banks of the leisurely Hudson opposite such
mansions as that of the Vanderbilts and, a little further up river, the Hyde
Park of the Roosevelts. But by weekends I had had a surfeit of magnificent
and massive trees, elegant landscapes, and the rigours of monastic life and
gladly boarded the Greyhound for the growing number of people a young
Englishman with a theological book, A *Church Renascent*, to his credit was
meeting through a circle of socially and culturally voracious New Yorkers.

My meeting with Gitta and our ensuing friendship have remained
in my memory, not as a continuing and developing narrative, but as a se-

ries of sharply etched cameos. We met through the diminutive and short-sighted grandson of Sir Edward Lutyens, the noted English architect who designed the British embassy in Washington, D.C.

David Lutyens, an Old Etonian, now studying at Yale in his early twenties, had written two volumes of the then popular genre of verse drama, one of which, *Mary Stuart*, had earned a foreword by T.S. Eliot. He impressed me most, though, by his blind faith in leaving the curb, say, on Fifth Avenue, and crossing through a sea of screeching and hooting cars and emerging on the other side unscathed and totally unconcerned.

His incessant babble was flecked with erudition and classical illusion. Only his questions were naive. He loudly and everywhere pronounced he was gay and had lovers of incredible beauty and nobility of character. I think, though, that such was rather an extension of his verse dramas, for I seriously doubt he had ever known sex save through his own hand.

His maternal grandfather was Chaim Weizmann, first president of Israel and a brilliant chemist, so David's inheritance was rich from both genetic streams. I saw him a year or so later in London, but shortly after that he dropped out of sight and a mutual woman friend, Nora, Countess Wydenbruck, who will appear later in the memoirs, told me that he had suffered a total breakdown and lost all knowledge of the English language, of which he had demonstrated such considerable prowess as well as prolixity.

At Yale he had made close friends of another woman, whom I later thought oddly reminiscent of Nora, and it was she who told David to put me, a fellow visiting Brit, in touch with a Gitta Sereny in New York City.

At the time I met her Gitta and her husband were much caught up in the vortex of the great photographic exhibition at the Museum of Modern Art, *The Family of Man*, which was curated by Edward Steichen.

I had a problem with Gitta, even though a friendship flowered very soon after I first sat in her spacious living room with the loquacious Lutyens. I knew I was a published author, and a writer of fiction, though I had no published evidence yet in that quarter to give me status.

I think similar thoughts moved in her Hungarian head (she told me she was part Esterhazy) of straight black hair, which was cut with a pixie-like fringe above an elfin visage. She had an almost exaggerated English accent, in spite of her Austro-Hungarian background, but then she had at-tended an English girls' boarding school. Whether that had provided her not only with the accent but also a hefty dollop of snobbery I don't know. But she was constantly harping on David Lutyens's illustrious ancestry and doing her best to ferret out my own.

She very quickly told me that she detested her mother and despised her bourgeois stepfather, who had been a minister in the Austrian government before the Anschluss and Hitler's henchmen took over. However, to give her due, there were many that she unequivocally admired. Among these was the violinist Yehudi Menuhin, whom she'd met while working with displaced children in war-torn Europe. There was also Steichen, of course, and dozens of others I have now forgotten. I should add, however, that there seemed to be *none* of low profile and with only commonplace achievements.

Her husband was both a charming and interesting figure. Out of Iowa, with a slow drawl commensurate with a seemingly unrufflable tem-perament, he was tall and gangling and a dead ringer for Gary Cooper, the movie star. He was ever attentive to Gitta's every whim and imperious command, though he would occasionally pause to smile and say that he thought she was being just a mite ridiculous. As often as not this would occur over their only child, a little boy named Christopher. Gitta was well protected from puerile claims by an Austrian au-pair-cum-nanny as well as a complaisant husband who happened also to be a fond daddy. Neverthe-less, she was not beyond seeking to include me in the battalion devoted to five-year-old Christopher's welfare.

One incident, however, put a stop to that. She asked me to take him for a short walk around two or three blocks and I reluctantly complied. Reluctantly because, I suspect, the child in me was too competitive to deal with that real one scowling up at me. We had never bonded. However, I did give in to her entreaties, as Don was nowhere near 101st Street and Riverside Drive, the boy's nanny was away somewhere, and Gitta had to be down at the Museum of Modern Art to help their friend Edward Ste-ichen in his preparations for the enormous *Family of Man* photographic exhibition that was scheduled to open in 1955.

At first all went well enough. Dressed against the freshness of a fall morning, little Christopher even let me hold his hand as we headed west and turned down Riverside Drive. It was when we reached our first and only traffic lights that trouble erupted. It was red as we arrived and I felt my arm stretch tight as my young companion still proceeded to march south. I gave his arm a yank.

"Whoa!" I shouted. "Light's still red."

"No traffic," he chirped.

"Doesn't matter. We wait for amber, then for green. *Then* we go."

"I wanna go now."

"Well, you can't."

"You stupid. No cars. Nothing. Now it's gone yellow. We still can go."

I clung firmly to the struggling fingers. "Well, we're not!"

"Why not? You stupid David."

"Why not is because I bloody well say *not*. And if you want more explanation, I'll knock that bloody beret off, if you don't do as you're told."

I could see his face wrinkle but resolutely refused to watch the summoning of puerile tears. When the lights blinked green I grabbed him across the street with such force that his little feet barely touched the ground.

He was silent all the way home — and stayed that way until, sitting at opposite ends of the living room, we both heard the key in the front door lock and his mother reappeared. With a howl he rushed to her and grabbed her, shrieking hysterically that I had been a nasty bully and forced him across the street when he didn't want to go.

I let all that farrago of nonsense exhaust itself before meeting her eye, prepared to reply. But she forestalled me. "Perhaps you didn't know, David, but Christopher has been taught that he will always receive a rational reply to his queries. An intelligent child is at least owed that."

I was ready with my response — which I don't think would be that much different now, more than fifty years later. "In the first place, his response to a traffic light didn't deserve an intelligent response — even if I understood the sequential mechanism of the bloody thing. And second, it is far more important that he learn early on how to deal with a *force majeure*. And they don't yield rational explanations. I told him what he was to do and that should have been enough. His life was in my hands and that was that."

After much more to and fro we agreed to disagree, as we did over so many of our differing opinions, for we were truly of separate worlds. One further example of that arose out of a generous gesture on her part. She was uneasy about my monastic setting and offered to find me a better (implying respectable) job in the city. She contacted an old buddy of Don's who was the editor-in-chief of a major paperback publishing house.

I went to see said gent and he offered me a junior editorial job — though only after making it quite clear that there would be sexual dues to be paid to him personally on my part. We compromised, when I declared there was nothing doing, by him allowing me to contribute blurbs and text précis for individual books on a freelance basis.

When I told Gitta of this she was furious — not for the financial details he agreed to pay but for the fact that her husband's college chum was homosexual and had never told her! Poor Gitta — that wasn't all she was never told. Don once said to me that he considered himself one of the most fortunate men in the New York world of fashion photography as exemplified by *Vogue*. For as a straight man, he told me, among a sea of gays, he could have the pick of dozens of women from both within the Condé Nast organization and without.

Gitta was avid to reveal her New York world to me and I'd be lying if I were to deny the pleasure I took when seated at her dinner table with the likes of Edward Steichen, Edward Weston, and less prestigious names but usually men (rarely women) that she would explain later were figures of enormous power and influence in their particular field.

She was also interested in improving my social techniques. I think that was what she had in mind when she secured me an invitation to join her for a champagne supper aboard the SS *Andrea Doria*, which was a charity benefit for the Metropolitan Opera. I spent a sizeable number of my saved American dollars to rent a tuxedo for that occasion. Imagine my gall (and Gitta's) when we arrived on board to find a large number of the men assembled wearing Bermuda shorts. It wasn't that I recalled but the ghastly decor in the first- and second-class lounges (a seasick green with something like spidery seaweed embedded between the glass on the cocktail tables), when, shortly after, we heard of the terrible tragedy of the liner sinking on the return portion of her maiden voyage.

I was never daunted by New York — it was too much a transatlantic London — but all cities suggest loneliness without the key of friends. And it was

Gitta more than anyone who provided just that. She was not only an open sesame to other people but in herself was a fascination. Quintessentially European, she carried the Continent as well as its twentieth-century scars in her person and I never ceased to love to listen to her stories of Vienna. (I have a suspicion that Max Reinhardt, the theatre maestro, screwed her, as he certainly was a major influence and her observations were intimate.)

But then that was the way with her. I was never surprised to learn that after our "brief encounter," as it were, she was to go on and become renowned as an author and TV figure in the United Kingdom as a result of her book and subsequent writings on the likes of Albert Speer, Hitler's friend and architect, whom she befriended and got to know in Spandau after his sentencing at Nuremberg.

She did (and obviously still does) possess the knack to squirm into the deepest recesses of a person's thoughts, particularly, I think, if guilt also lies there. That activity may seem congruous with a now elderly woman for whom time has not been kind. Always petite, she has now shrunk and her elfin features have shrivelled. She looks from the distortion of a TV screen like a witch. But it was not a witch I knew in her obscurity, only a vital woman desperately concerned to make sense of a chaotic world and to come to grips with the nature of human evil. It would seem she has triumphantly accomplished her purpose.

If I end on a mildly negative note it is only because I refuse to lie to myself in these recollections. When Floyd and I went to visit her and her family in Kensington (she had now included a second child, a daughter born in England) I was eager to show my beloved professor off to my close friend in those New York days when he and I were separated by the kind of cosmic politics (North Korean communism) that intrigued her, and vice versa. But this arch-liberal, this so collected woman who could look the personal ramifications of Nazism in the face, confront the reality of little children in the death camps and the plight of those un-killed who wandered homeless, couldn't cope with the simple reality of two men in love. It was another coolness she displayed then, polite but repudiating, as she remained at arm's length. Alas.

# 10
# GLIMPSES OF HUMAN MANHATTAN

Maxwell Bodenheim: I met him in a bar on the Lower West Side, not too far from the General Theological Seminary in late spring of 1953. Also present was my host, W.H Auden, and at a neighbouring table, raucously drunk, sat Dylan Thomas, whom I had recently seen in California at Stanford where he had been amiably misbehaving, and who was to be dead before summer's end. My irritation with that man (though certainly not with his poetry, which I love to read aloud before an audience) was hardly his fault. It was that whenever I followed in his raucous, alcoholic wake, I was so often confused with him — even being addressed as "Mr. Thomas." This mistaken identity, despite the fact that he was donkey's years older, that I was closer to being teetotal, that I had a Cornish rather than a Welsh background, and that our looks were only a mite similar (the hair, perhaps?), nigh drove me mad. And I might add that the confusion continued long after his death and I had reached his age in Canada where I continued to read him before selected audiences in our home.

Max Bodenheim was not drunk — but was obviously anxious to rectify the situation as soon as possible. Then I was already getting the impression that the luminaries of American letters generally achieved their genesis under the fumes of alcohol.

There was something else quintessentially American about him but this attracted rather than repelled. There was nothing oblique about him. His voice was as flat as his manners and he exuded his country's insistence to "cut the crap." In the same vein was the national determination to resist all "bullshit." He might have been a transplanted Southerner, become the Poet of Greenwich Village and a famous local Bohemian and fiery adversary of his peers, but he was simply "All-American" in my then so British eyes.

His own bloodshot ones steadily regarded me before he essayed a friendly conversation. "Who the fuck are you, kid? And what you starin' at me for?"

I came on like a cross between a British Airways commercial and Julie Andrews. "I'm just visiting New York and doing a bit of sightseeing." I wanted him to know that I knew who he was without letting on that Wystan had given me an acid-laced verbal snapshot of his fellow poet. "You sure live in a thrilling city, Mr. Bodenheim."

The result was unexpected. "And you're sure full of shit! Where'd you say you were from?"

I wasn't going to give the bastard a chance to fool around with my accent, so I said, "I'm from 103rd Street and Riverside Drive."

"Then what the fuck you talking about New York City for? It stops at 42nd Street, didn't you know? After that is just a goddamn pit. Not that I've been up that far to look in. They tell me it's full of the fucking rich. So there's another reason to stay here — even if you have to share the Village with more and more assholes." His gaze enveloped my table with his hostile stare at that juncture, but we were saved development by an almost girlish shriek from Dylan Thomas of "Goddamn Yanks!" as he rose unsteadily before sailing from the dim bar into an unwelcome daylight.

Beatrice Von Scharbert: Bebe's story lies half in New Haven, but as I met her in Manhattan and she spent much of her time escaping the university town, where her father was a renowned professor, for the big city, she equally belongs here. She is also here because I have used her extensively in my fiction — not least in my short story collection *The Connecticut Countess* and in the title story in particular.

As her maiden name indicates she came from an aristocratic German family, but in some ways she was a Frieda Lawrence and always in rebellion against her blood inheritance. She patently made it a point to befriend gays — to an almost unhealthy degree when it came to arranging sexual trysts for them. One of her best friends was the near recluse playwright Thornton Wilder, who also resided in New Haven, and she had many tales to tell of him and, if I recall correctly, his twin brother.

Rebel or not, that didn't prevent Bebe from marrying an Italian prince and bearing him a son before they went their separate ways. I never met her child, but I do recall her telling me that bringing up an extremely handsome son in Italy presented several problems. One she cited was keeping men from investigating his person when he accompanied her in his early teens to the cinema.

Bebe had a great sense of humour and was always chortling. She also favoured adventure, whether in bold conversation — such as at the sumptuous dinners she liked to give — or in more intimate circumstances, when she had a distinct penchant to drink too much. It was on one such occasion, when we were alone in her New Haven apartment, that, having persuaded me to consume prodigious quantities of Heidsieck champagne, she fell upon my prostrate person and managed to successfully suck my cock: the only woman in my life to do so.

Although so keen to smile, her laughter was often bitter. In truth she was rather an unhappy person in spite of her comfortable circumstances, or perhaps because of them. As it was a time for me of relative poverty I sometimes found her moods difficult to comprehend, let alone put up with. She really nursed an active dislike of America, even though her ancient mother was a true patriot whose lineage extended back to the *Mayflower*. But then Europe spelled both her father's stiff family and the familial obligations arising from her marriage and motherhood — neither of which she could abide. So there she was, a witty, wealthy island of moral irresponsibility and loneliness behind the bubbly facade.

No wonder she was drawn to the marginalized such as gays in denial or full of self-hate, or those upper-crust Europeans cast on the shore of the vast democracy into which they found it so difficult to assimilate. In that context she perhaps fulfilled a positive purpose, selling laughter (however wry) for tears and providing a peep of luxury to those who would not otherwise ever see it. In her fashion and mine, we loved each other.

Frank McGregor of Harper & Brothers: I suppose "Mac" was the first prosperous gay gent I was to meet in the United States. He was certainly archetypal. There was the apartment on Gramercy Park (said to have once belonged to Stanford White); the weekend cottage in Kent, Connecticut; and the place in Guatemala, which I never visited.

He also had the standard boyfriend, atypically perhaps, called only by his surname, but nearly always drunk by noon and thus another sight then unfamiliar to me. But I include Mac in my pantheon of those who wittingly or unwittingly have accorded me contours, mental and emotional, because I grew a little more cynical, a little more realistic perhaps, over the adult world I had started to inhabit.

To start with he was a man who eminently looked of consequence. He turned out to be yet another Canadian, in his case from Nova Scotia, who had gone south to better his life. He had the kind of handsome Anglo-Saxon looks that the French, for instance, favour on their upper-class magazines and comparable advertising. He was tall, with a fine head of grey hair, blue eyes, and a slim bod that was invariably clad in suits and other garments such as seersucker jackets from Brooks Brothers.

An elegant man, then, and with a mobile mouth in consort with those flashing blue eyes, he was someone who gave a distinct impression of intelligence and culture. The latter he had in spades, but I do not think now that he was a particularly bright man.

Clever enough, to be sure, to rise to the presidency of the distinguished publishing house of Harper & Brothers and someone who could claim not just a business relationship but a measure of friendship with the likes of Aldous Huxley, Sinclair Lewis, and William Faulkner. All the same, I sensed some kind of intellectual con game from the start. I had been passed on to him by, I think, Gitta Sereny, and he made it perfectly clear from the outset that he regarded me as sexual provender, just as I made clear to him that I sought a publisher for my first novel, and, failing that, perhaps a job with the firm.

In the event, neither satisfied the other but over several months we did get to know each other fairly well and I became, albeit briefly, a part of his weekend entourage to the Connecticut cottage in the company of his besotted lover and his various acquaintances, like the poet Gene Baro, who when he wasn't back in his native New York looked after the Florida estate of Marjorie Kinnan Rawlings, the novelist and author of *The Yearling*. I was to meet up again with Gene (after he unsuccessfully pursued me on one of those weekends, while his artist lover pretended nothing was happening) on my return to London, so I will come back to him when I reach that chronological section of these pages.

By the time that Jewish Gene was lazily looking for a little erotic weekend divertissement chez Mac, the latter and I were discussing at length both British and American literature, particularly the novel, and even more particularly from him the living authors thereof. But rarely did my host rise above plain gossip and commonplace observation. Time and time again I was roused to the point of frenzy in frustration when I asked about T.S. Eliot's intellectual background before his becoming an ardent Anglo-Catholic, of how rooted in the Midwest was Sinclair Lewis or how rooted was Faulkner in Mississippi. But all I got was who was straight and who was gay, and how I should read up-and-coming writers such as his favourite, Glenway Westcott, who was now a Harper author — also insinuating that I too could follow in such footsteps if only I were more obliging.

Of course I was a prig and well on the way to being an intellectual snob. But from Eric Abbott to Wystan Auden, people had started appetites in me and I was burning to replete them and become one day a rounded figure with my own personalized repository of knowledge that could effectively feed my pen. I did not believe then as I do now that an excess of intellectuality is alien to the truly effective novelist. The charge that my youthful hero, D.H. Lawrence, made against Bertrand Russell, of too much brain obscuring vital emotional truth, remains as true today for fiction as it did then. Frank McGregor made me ache for the rigours and challenge of the academy. But thank God I was soon out of his vortex and returned to England, where I was destined to meet a number of radically different people.

# 11

# DEREK PATMORE AND
# FRANK RUDMAN

During a relatively brief period in my life, Derek Patmore taught me some hard lessons of literary history — especially in the context of the virtues and vices of the British class system. With Derek it is hard to know where to start. Perhaps at the very end when I had grown to love him and become his literary executor. He died in a Dublin nursing home, nursed by nuns but very much alone and intestate.

We met — as I met so many — during those two intense years I sojourned in London in the mid-1950s. I had secured a job — on a probationary level — as a radio producer with the BBC's *Third Programme*. He was passed on to me by my immediate boss, the novelist P.H. Newby (*Picnic at Sakkara*, etc.), partly, I now believe, as a mild act of hostility, as Derek had a reputation for endlessly bombarding the BBC with futile program ideas and Howard Newby, although affirmative on my selection board, afterwards always felt negative to my "gaydar." He was a dapper though disappointed shortish man, made super-aware (mainly by being patronized) at the BBC of his proletarian origins and lack of a university degree.

He also made me very sensible to the fact that his books had not received a positive response in North America. In fact I'm inclined to think he only agreed to my few months' trial as a producer because he thought I might help him secure a New York publisher through all the contacts I had left behind me, such as Frank McGregor and Cass Canfield of Harper & Brothers, and John Farrar of Farrar, Strauss and Young (as it then was), and the editor of the paperback house that Gitta Sereny had introduced me to. For the record, I also invented a few names during those three successive interview boards when, to the impatience of the rest of the board, he persisted in questioning me exclusively in that context, which had little or nothing to do with my abilities as a potential producer.

I probably took Derek to lunch on the generous expenses the corporation accorded its producers for the purpose of acquiring new broadcasters — in my case to give "Talks" of a serious nature, although not restricted as to subject. Derek was a talker rather than a giver of formal talks, and I soon learned, whenever my attention was tempted to wander, to listen for the perpetual "my dear," which signified the end of a torrent or the start of a new one.

All the same, Derek, dear, dumb, well-meaning Derek, was stuff-full of interesting matter. The great-grandson of Coventry Patmore (*The Angel in the House*) and rival of Tennyson, his family was moneyed as well as living within the right literary echelons. His mother, Brigit, a great Irish beauty in her youth, had been the lover of Richard Aldington and through him a member of the D.H. Lawrence circle. That fascinated me, of course, as a disciple of Lawrence's, and I felt I was truly encountering living history when I sat in her and Derek's basement apartment in Notting Hill and heard her talk of "Lorenzo" and of the famous photo when they had all bathed nude together in southern France.

By this time, however, such romantic days were over and Brigit's idea of glamour was a visit to the Notting Hill Gate cinema for a Saturday matinee. One vivid cameo summoning up both her fascinating past and her penurious present occurred just prior to Christmas that same year. I was there with her and her devoted son, Derek, when the door leading to the area steps was knocked on. When Derek opened it, it was to reveal a liveried chauffeur who handed him a small package. It was a jar of caviar from Harrods sent by Dame Rebecca West, an old pal from earlier days. One can only hope that Dame Rebecca was wholly ignorant of her friend's present-day circumstances and thus the sheer inappropriateness of such a gift.

Derek was the almost-stereotypical gay son of a doting mother. His younger brother, Michael, a successful advertising man, was often irritated with him because, not only did Derek never buckle to a serious, well-paying job, but he and his mother shared laughs together over those unfortunate if wealthy members of the bourgeoisie who were doomed to earn money but were never at home in their own beloved and happily restricted world of the arts.

Derek Patmore was a gossip to easily outclass most of the genre. I loved his unmalicious anecdotes and when he told me of his wartime exploits as a journalist (could it have really been for the *Times?*) posted to neutral Turkey. He was asked first by MI5 to do a little amateur spying for them, and then (mystifyingly) asked by the Germans to do likewise for their side. He had no intention of doing that, of course, but in the event it didn't matter. He soon developed such an impressive reputation not only as a gossip but as a disseminator of secrets that all the intelligence agencies based in and around espionage-ridden Ankara avoided him like the plague!

In London, with me, more than ten years later, it was not quite the same. From his wide net of acquaintances he introduced me to many — Derek was utterly generous in this as in so much else — but the results were not always quite satisfactory. For instance, we were sauntering down Piccadilly, just past Burlington House, when he grabbed my arm and said, "My dear, let's see if Graham is home."

Before I knew what was happening, he was knocking at the door of some ancient and ritzy apartments and a rather flustered balding man eventually appeared.

"What the hell!" he began (or something to that effect). "Oh, it's you, Derek. What on earth do you want?"

"Can we come in, Graham — I do so hate making introductions on doorsteps." With that my friend advanced forward with a bewildered Graham Greene retreating before him. When we were in the comfortable living room, Derek started up again. "I wanted to introduce you, Graham, to my little Cornish genius."

As I squirmed, the author of *The Heart of the Matter* scowled. Indeed, the face of Graham Greene didn't lighten — nor did he ask us to sit down — as Derek explained my unpublished and callow novel, *Finger in the Deep*, and my BBC status to the Master, who, I thought at one point in Derek's extended spiel, was himself seeking to escape his own dwelling.

When we were finally outside, the shame lapping now about my earlobes, I remonstrated to Derek for obtruding so on the man's privacy. But Derek, long used to rejection of every sort, made light of it. I do believe he saw it all as some kind of success — in that Graham Greene would talk up my novel to his publishers, that I would get the author to do a "Talk" for the *Third Programme*, and that he himself would somehow benefit as the instigator of the whole business. Then Derek believed in a benevolent deity, only too keen to help the descendant of a pious Catholic convert such as Coventry Patmore.

And there were indeed times when such credence on his part seemed justified. I cannot conclude these reminiscences without referring to the time when Derek visited Floyd and me at our home in Vancouver in the 1960s. His fare had been paid by yet another publisher — he went through many — who perhaps had been impressed by his biography of Coventry Patmore or, perhaps yet more significantly, the several travel books to his credit. At any rate, he arrived joyfully *chez nous* to begin collecting notes for the book on Canada he had been commissioned to write.

With that project in mind we proceeded to show him local landmarks and people that might perhaps be of use in his book. He was certainly a success with our friends, such as the noted artists John Koerner, Gordon Smith, and Jack Shadbolt and their respective spouses and families. How they would have fared in his pages, alas, we shall never know. The clue to that I think lies in the fact that when we took him to Squamish along the snaking coast ride that bites into the mountain flank of the Coastal Range and past the thunderous waters of Shannon Falls, dear Derek was too busy titillating us with the latest London gossip even to glance out of the car window.

In vain did eagles soar above us, ravens glide over the thin surf of the inlet: Derek saw nothing; heard nothing. It was likewise driving through the stands of giant cedar in first-growth forest, to the charms of Victoria and the sight of killer whales in their pod as we journeyed by ferry. Derek was oblivious to all but humankind, especially those who were disposed to listen to him. But such was presumably inadequate for the publisher seeking a travel book, for one by Derek on Canada never appeared.

I have a suspicion that the experience was not new for Derek. But by this time I knew that the rejection wouldn't depress him for more than a moment or two. Then my Micawber-like friend would shrug, and in later years give a fond hug to his beloved — if totally un-housetrained — pug, Sonia, and start life all over again. That alone was a lesson worth emulating.

Frank Rudman represented — on a cheery if beery note — my London swansong. Frank was to the streets of his London what Maxwell Bodenheim had been to New York. And both knew every watering place available to them.

I met him just at the end of my BBC episode. He was in fact my immediate boss at the small press of Ace Books. We made a merry gay team, sharing a peculiar competence in recalling novels that we could reproduce in mass paperback form. My first was Doris Lessing's *The Grass Is Singing*, and we were mutually horrified at the garish cover it subsequently wore. I have been ashamed ever since to meet Mrs. Lessing, who is an author, her science fiction stuff aside, I profoundly admire.

Further embarrassment came my way when Frank reluctantly persuaded an even more reluctant me to do an editing job on a western involving a cowboy hero who becomes an agent of justice and retribution in the Far West when he sets out to rescue a young Easterner who has become corrupted by the wild and woolly life he has found west of the Mississippi. A hefty excision was made of an early portion of the novel, which seemed preoccupied, indeed bogged down in superficial detail, with a love affair in Philadelphia between a rich young woman and the book's hero. That was fatal surgery, for it provided the sole motivation for why said hero should defend the weak and wayward young man who was facing disaster in the lawless West.

To the horror of both of us, when our south coast rep arrived one day and announced that our "gay" western was selling like hotcakes — indeed, better than any other title on his list — it only then dawned on us what I'd done. I forget (honest!) the title of the book and its author, but I never forgot the lesson of arbitrary editing, and my distaste of reduced or "digest" books remains as forceful today as it ever was.

Frank was a "character" of a kind you'd expect to find in London (at least in the mid-1950s) and probably nowhere else on the globe save, perhaps, New York. He sported a ridiculously extravagant Oxford accent (acquired, he once drunkenly told me, from an old lover), was never seen without his bowler hat, and was as keen on his fresh carnation buttonhole as Prime Minister Pierre Elliott Trudeau was to be some years later.

He was a little man, always formally dressed, and always faithful to his own created image of a London businessman with a bizarre artistic bent. As I've suggested, he was also as gay as a hoot owl. Unfortunately, he was also a total alcoholic. Being an innately humorous man he could make even that affliction disarming. Once when visiting friends of mine his consumption of beer made him suddenly incontinent over the factory floor, where a score or more West Indian immigrant garment workers could observe the growing pool. Then there was something altogether in-continent about that image of a bowler hat hovering about a pub bar with the always flamboyant but sometimes wilted carnation perched starkly above that protuberant beer tummy usually grey with its owner's cigarette ash. Not a pretty sight, you say? I still miss him. Embarrassment or not, he still spells London, just as much as St. Paul's or the Tower — where in former years he would probably have ended up.

# 12
# NORA WYDENBRUCK

F ew in my life went from rather daunting acquaintance to warm friend so quickly as did Nora Wydenbruck. My ultra snobby friend, Alberto de Lacerda, a Portuguese poet and translator of Edith Sitwell into Portuguese, whom I met in true London fashion, through Derek Patmore, introduced me to Nora — but not before giving me an extended social and literary pedigree! The Countess Nora Wydenbruck was the German translator of T.S. Eliot and a niece of the Princess Maria von Thurn und Taxis, who owned the Castle of Duino, where the poet Rainer Maria Rilke wrote his famous elegies.

A story arises right out of this very data. Some years later, I was being interviewed in Canada and brashly spouted all that verbiage. When the magazine article appeared so did the following sentence: "Watmough knew all the greats including the German poet Rilke." I need hardly point out that Rilke died the year of my birth — 1926! So much for name-dropping.

Alberto, whose social horizons had been set as frequent visitor at that period (the mid-1950s) to Renishaw, the stately home of the Sitwells in the English Midlands, was an expert in "filling me in" on aspects of Nora, including some comments to the effect that all these old dames seemed to take a shine to up-and-coming young queers.

To me, at least, Nora never came on as an "old dame" and certainly never made the slightest allusion as to my sexual proclivities. What this London-born (1884) Austrian, whose father was the First Secretary of the Austrian Embassy at the Court of St. James, had in common with me was a religious conviction, a love of literature, and a penchant for hard work. I may have worked on a farm, milking cows, scattering dung, and the like; Nora, when times were tough between the wars, cheerfully worked as a waitress in the Lyons chain of tea shops in London.

The prior information that Alberto had fed me as we walked from my rooms on Ladbroke Grove to the nearby West Kensington home on Addison Gardens of the Countess included her reputation as a social hostess. Alberto said she gave beautiful dinner parties for small numbers who included the known and the unknown, European princesses, and peasant monks — her only yardstick being their ability to contribute lively conversation. These candlelit dinner parties took place in the ornately brocaded basement of 13 Addison Road, where the walls were replete with splendid large canvases by her silver-haired and courtly husband, the Bavarian-born Alfons Purtscher, whose forte was the painting of pedigree horses.

I attended some of those dinners, but for the most part on such occasions the other guests were either impoverished young women from Austria, many of them relatives, or a scattering of priests and laity from the Catholic purlieus of Kensington. More often, I walked over to her place for drinks upstairs in the living room, and as Nora puffed away at her cigarettes, we would discuss everything from the pope to literary London. I sensed that, like me, she was keen to publish more of her own stuff and not exist only as T.S. Eliot's translator. Indeed, that was a bond between us.

There was also that of family. She loved to hear about my Cornish background, of my widely differing parents and my equally different two brothers for that matter. She was obviously in love with her husband, Alfons, and proud of not only his painting but his equally dexterous skills with tapestry and his ability to repair the brocade of the faded and worn furniture that she had inherited from her Hapsburg past. Her one lament, it seemed, was over her son, who although a successful ship's captain somewhere out on the oceans, was apparently utterly uninterested in her literary world or his father's painterly one. But I was only allowed to peek at such matters; Nora did not indulge her deepest emotions in public.

One of her happiest decisions on my behalf was to hold a garden party for me to meet people such as my co-religionist Tom Eliot, as well as a few other literary luminaries she thought might interest me and hopefully vice versa. On the day in question she told me to stay at first indoors in her sitting room and leave matters to her. Nora was nothing but masterful and, I'm convinced, incapable of dithering.

I was examining a large bowl of waxed fruit when she ushered in a tall, sleek-haired gent with a soft voice and gentle smile. I dropped a false pear back whence it came as I put out my own trembling hand to join his firm one. In a way I suppose the meeting was a disappointing one. There was I dying to talk of *The Wasteland*, *Four Quartets*, and his recent plays such as *The Cocktail Party* and *The Confidential Clerk*. But all the Nobel Prize winner wished to discuss was the difficulty of finding adequate servers and sidemen at his parish church, the inadequacy of clerical incomes, and the general difficulties confronting such Anglo-Catholic parishes as St. Cyprian's, Clarence Gate. It was apparent that Nora had informed him only too well of our mutual religious sympathies and that had immediately engaged him. But my literary aches were something the great man was not reasonably disposed to discuss at a friend's house on a purely social occasion.

There was more promising material outside in the garden, where after some half-hour or so we joined the other guests. Those standing chatting on the tiny lawn under a pallid London sun included the poet and journalist Stephen Spender, the sinologist and translator Arthur Waley, the Mozambique-born son of a Portuguese diplomat Alberto de Lacerda, and the poet-publisher John Lehman, whom I was able to use on one of my *Third Programme* literary panels before I left the employ of the BBC.

Several of the above deserve chapters for themselves, as our acquaintanceship grew — although not always pleasantly. With Nora, though, the more we saw the more we liked. It was not only the "John Blunt" in her that appealed but her total refusal to admit defeat. I don't know whether I was like that myself then, but, sure as God, that was what I wanted to be!

She reminded me of Natalie Guthrie in her simple dress code: usually a tweed costume, a woollen sweater, and a rope of pearls. There were probably variants but that is what I remember vividly during those endless sessions when she would describe her girlhood back in Imperial Austria (memories that subsequently inspired several short stories of mine) and

I fed her interest in the occupants of the house in which I was living. St. Basil's House, a large Victorian dwelling, was owned by the Fellowship of St. Alban and St. Sergius, an Anglican/Orthodox foundation to encourage ecumenicity between Canterbury, Constantinople, and Moscow — the three patriarchal Sees. That, of course, left out the largest and most influential — the See of Rome. But we lived, perforce, within the inherited wounds in the Body of Christ. Ecumenically minded Nora could see the implications of such first steps — even though so many more are still needed to fulfill Jesus' own wish "that they may be one."

St. Basil's House was efficiently run by two ladies: one Greek Orthodox, the other High Anglican. Other inhabitants included a French-born Orthodox archimandrite. Father Lev was a scholar, an eccentric, and a holy clown. He attended Quaker services as often as not on Sundays. He came from a French military family and was himself a chaplain to the French Army before he left Roman Catholicism for Orthodoxy. He told me that he had witnessed the last execution by guillotine in the French Army. He also knew weird and wonderful people from around the world. He had taught (I think) in Beirut, and in any event he was as knowledgeable of Lebanon as he was of Greece and Turkey, indeed of all Europe. He had also served as an interpreter with the British forces in the First World War! And consequently his near-perfect English was sprinkled with cusswords that he used without pausing for breath or change of vocal tone. He insisted I speak French with him and was a harsh judge of my limitations.

Also in the house lived a young Anglican priest who was wedded to his motorbike, a rather forlorn young bisexual man who had been pantingly pursued by a famous literary critic in Bristol and then fallen in love with a beautiful young blond woman who was unfortunately (for him) headed for a nunnery. And then, of course, there was me.

I lived at St. Basil's for the whole of my London stay, and among the many visitors, I met a variety of Russians, clerical and lay. Among the former was the local parish priest, Father Anthony, who claimed to be something of a spiritual pundit — though not impressing me as such. Among his claims to fame was the story that when being interviewed on the BBC about the size of the Russian Orthodox community in London he said, "We are not yet a million." The reality was that there were only a few thousand.

What so many of them had in common was the ability to fall out with one another. Last week's bosom friend was this week's archenemy! I had never met such a rancorous bunch and those antics alone kept Countess Nora in fits of laughter.

Until 2003 I was still in Christmas card touch with Joan, the jolly Anglican hostess of the Fellowship. Her partner is now deceased but she herself later married a bishop and with him subsequently "poped" and now live in Roman Catholic retirement among other elderly.

Chain-smoking Nora still pokes bony fingers in my ribs to remind me of down-to-earth reality — even if it is from beyond the grave.

# 13
## BESSIE SULLIVAN

I don't think that even her most loving friends would have described Bessie as an Albert Einstein of her gender. Nevertheless she had a Yankee shrewdness from her Buffalo, New York, origins, possibly honed by her later experience as a wealthy young heiress in Ontario. And she certainly had a sense of fiscal preservation that stood her in good stead when she frequently fished among the weeds of literary deadbeats, sycophants, and general hangers-on for her dinner or luncheon guests on London's posh Eaton Square, where she was neighbour to such as the playwright Terence Rattigan and Randolph Churchill.

I met her through a friend of Derek Patmore, a bookseller whom Bessie patronized as she was always buying on Monday the books she had seen reviewed in the *Observer* and *Sunday Times* the previous day. I doubt whether she ever got through any of them but they found a prominent place on her coffee table until the next batch was purchased.

Before condemning her we might recall that by such gestures a small but distinct contribution to the book business in London was sustained.

Here are some further facts about her that are pertinent to my recollections of the diminutive, white-haired, coiffed, and altogether elegant lady with the carefully studied voice and self-conscious gestures that involved her ubiquitous cane.

Bessie (neé Hees) was the widow of Montreal-born Alan Sullivan (1868–1947), whose father had been bishop of Algoma. He was an engineer who also made a reputation as both a fiction and non-fiction writer of material drawn from the Canadian North, which he knew well. He won a Governor General's Award with his novel *Three Came to Ville Marie* but has been virtually ignored by the Canadian literati, as he was nothing if not grotesquely politically incorrect. One asinine encyclopedia entry I refuse to identify describes his fifty books as "Anglocentric and socially hierarchical," which makes them sound like a cross between Who's Who and the Holy Bible.

Their four children were well planted in society. The eldest boy, a naval officer during the Second World War, was gay and died accidentally from a cigarette fire he ignited in his chalet in Kitzbühel. Bessie's eldest daughter was married to the governor of Algeria under Charles de Gaulle. Another was married to Liddell Hart, the military historian, and a further son was head of the German division of the BBC at Bush House and subsequently became a highly respected sinologist.

At Bessie's Sunday lunches on Eaton Square, attended by her faithful if acrimonious housekeeper, Giulietta, she had whichever guests her scalp-hunting instincts as a hostess managed to capture. I recall Cecil Roberts, author of *Victoria Four-Thirty* and an irascible old fart, and the daughter of John Galsworthy, who was so genteel she almost choked on her own refinement.

But with all her hostess pretension the sharp, shrewd Yankee still peeped through. Her mildly fake British accent obscured for some her ability to spot a phony a mile off. She did, though, worship success. I cannot remember how many times she reminded me that her nephew, George Alexander Drew, had been premier of Ontario. Then that was maybe something to do with the fact that we Canadians are always finding ourselves, when in foreign parts, in situations where those around us know nothing about the people we are referring to — and, stingingly, couldn't care less!

Bessie was brave, even stoic, over her close relatives — especially if they were drunks or gay or merely not famous. She wasn't afraid of circumlocutions. Referring to a beloved gay grandson, she informed me that he had "that thing that men get."

But it wasn't all euphemism with her. Once, when alone at table, I happened to kick her shin with my leg. I was at once full of apology — until she told me to shut up, as it was her wooden leg I'd accidentally kicked. Maybe it was metal. I forget now. But only her Italian housekeeper, Giulietta, would furnish the details. Her family shut up like a clam if that gammy leg was even mentioned. When the chips were down, in spite of her years and years as a U.K. resident, she was still the forthright North American blithely speaking the unmentionable, while her family were circumspect Brits, all obliqueness and embarrassed silences.

Bessie liked to talk about the past and I was always the attentive listener. She and her husband, Alan, had back in the 1920s befriended the then young novelist and short story writer H.E. Bates. He was, she said, of a very poor background, and he had done much of his early writing in a shed in their Kentish garden. The allusion touched a soft spot in me because the very first book I gave Floyd for his birthday when we separated in 1952 (me teaching school in Aldershot, England, he returned to Stanford to work for his doctorate) was Bates's *Love for Lydia*, which had special appeal to our then so romantic propensities.

Another, if mildly grating, indication of Bessie's hard-headedness occurred when I was about to leave England for the last time as resident and was destined never to see her again. A friend I had met through John Lehman, the young novelist and biographer of J.B. Priestley, David Hughes, had somehow gotten his own publisher to agree for me to ghost the adventures of a young man named Churchill who had joined the French Foreign Legion. He claimed to be a relative of *the* Churchill, but as I sat and listened to his accounts of life in North Africa my doubts as to his verisimilitude began to grow. However, I was booked on the *Queen Elizabeth* to New York and sent the manuscript off to the publisher before I could receive payment for my efforts. It was Bessie who vouchsafed to lend me my fare back to Floyd — until such time as I was paid and could refund her. It was a month or two after I'd taken up residence in California that I learned *Life of Legionnaire* had been turned down and that consequently I'd receive no monies. Within the very same week came a curt letter from Bessie demanding her loan be returned. With a little scrambling we were able to satisfy her request, but there was no subsequent correspondence between us.

# 14
# GILBERT HARDING

It is certainly the BBC I have to thank for introducing me to this odd character. But as is so often the case, it soon developed that we had several threads of connection from both our pasts. But first a paragraph or two about who he was and what he did. It is an oddity of our era that someone can be known and physically recognizable by literally millions of people yet not only unheard of elsewhere but also forgotten and ignored in less than a generation within the context he or she was once a household name.

Such a case, I believe, would be that of Gilbert Harding, whose public persona as a curmudgeonly clown yet possessing of a certain erudition was virtually created by the BBC through the numerous and popular radio and TV programs and panels on which he appeared. He claimed to be born in a workhouse — which his father had administered. He certainly attended Cambridge University, as Eric Abbott, dean of Westminster, remembered him fondly as an Anglican long before his Roman Catholic days, and told me that Gilbert had been a pious if tormented undergraduate. I know nothing of the former but he was certainly full of tempestuous torment in the months I could claim to know him fairly well.

He agreed to do a radio panel show for me that centred on the likes of him and the urbane *Punch* author Basil Boothroyd, who were to ask probing questions of foreigners who had settled in the country about their opinions of Britain and the British. For my pilot program (and it never got beyond that!) I asked George Mikes, the diminutive Hungarian author of the bestselling humorous book *How to Be an Alien*. Unfortunately Gilbert read "probing" as "hostile" – with the result that Mikes became tearful, Gilbert lost his temper (a stock in trade with him), and Basil Boothroyd exemplified the kind of firm social rectitude that the British insist on maintaining when someone has loudly farted.

Oddly enough, I became friends with Gilbert Harding from then on – though one might compare it to friendship with a reasonably amiable tiger. Like W.H. Auden, Gilbert displayed an avid interest in my father – compared, that is, to my mother. Conversations at Broadcasting House, where he seemed to spend almost as much time as I did, invariably began with a question about my dad's welfare, but that done, he returned to an easier topic, namely, himself.

My new experience as a producer put me in a novel situation: how much were the people I was now meeting responding to me personally, and how much was their friendship only germane to my role? I had once asked Wystan Auden whether he thought that people who sought him out and claimed friendship were doing so because of his status and reputation rather than for himself. His reply was that he would never ask such a stupid question but if he discovered that a person was pretending to like him per se, when in fact the motives were self-serving, then that person would be dropped forever! Then I wasn't Wystan Auden, nor did I have either his moral stamina or his enormous reputation as a poet.

I did feel that Gilbert Harding quite liked me, and although he, too, was gay, he never made a pass or anything of the sort. And after all, he was firmly entrenched in his broadcasting status and, as a celebrity, was guaranteed a measure of sexual success. One weekend he invited me down to Brighton. It so happened that another friend of mine, Frank Rudman, was also spending that weekend in the coastal resort with his older lover. We arranged to meet if possible – given Gilbert's schedule and arrangements for me. That we did – and precipitately at that – was a surprise to us both.

When I got off the train and took a taxi to the spacious apartment, it was to be greeted by two young men, one who identified himself as Gilbert's personal secretary, the other as his personal servant. The latter showed me to my room, and it was only after that I joined my host and his secretary in the beautifully apportioned and furnished living room. Gilbert had indeed come a long way from his workhouse birthplace!

I may have been too preoccupied with taking in those lavish surroundings or merely nervous of being with this large, rather portly man with his bristling moustache for the space of a whole weekend. But after his opening comments about my journey on the *Brighton Belle* from London, I blithely took from my pocket a letter that I had recently received from my dad that elaborated on how he was recovering from his heart attack, which had felled him on the St. Enodoch golf course and where only his little grandson had been present to fetch help.

"You might be interested in this," I began — and started to read. The reaction was devastating.

"Who the hell wants to hear about your bloody father?" he began. "I certainly don't."

I was tongue-tied; would have remained so longer if he hadn't continued to berate me.

"Do you really think I invited you down here to hear about your bloody family, you little shit?"

I finally found my Cornish tantrum: "I don't know what your bloody motives were for asking me — though I certainly don't have to sit here and listen to your drunken spouting." I had noted the half-tumbler of what I presumed was Scotch at his side. When I reached the antechamber where I had first met his employees, George and Ted, George, his valet, pleaded for me to sit down. Secretary Ted then joined us. They both apologized at once. "He hasn't taken his pills. He's always like this when he forgets or refuses to take them. It isn't the drink — though that doesn't help."

"Well, I won't just sit there while he yells at me. I don't need that shit! I've got other people I can stay with. I'll take a hotel if they can't."

"He'll never forgive himself tomorrow if you go. Please, Mr. Watmough, give us a chance. Let Ted here try just once more. Gilbert's more likely to listen to him than anyone else."

I sat there sullenly for five minutes or so, when Ted returned to the doorway and beckoned me to follow him back to the living room. It was as if nothing had happened. I could only presume Gilbert had taken his medication and that it had instantly worked. I certainly didn't make mention of my family. Nor did he. I've forgotten exactly what we did talk about, but when we were sitting *à deux* in the snug but elegant dining room with upholstered walls, he did ring a buzzer under his end of the rosewood table and call for Ted. To me he said, "I have to take so many of these bloody pills that I sometimes forget. If that happens I get rather grumpy and I wouldn't want you to see that."

I said nothing, but when Ted had reassured him and departed I got him to talk of his mental/emotional condition. Once his suspicions were allayed and he could see I was quite serious, he poured forth what a bane to his life it all was. He went on to ruefully acknowledge that his very contumacy that had led to his fame as a broadcaster was due to his neuroses. After that came an immense sadness as he described himself as a nothing who had achieved false fame, and then he started to cry. I got up and held his large head in my hands. I felt I was trying to still the sobs of not the current most famous comic figure in the British Isles but the disconsolate clown in Leoncavallo's opera, *Pagliacci*. For me, at least, it was a moment of learning.

Before I returned to London that weekend Gilbert introduced me in the Greyhound pub to the New Zealand writer Hector Bolitho, as the latter's Cornish name intrigued me, meaning, rather significantly I was about to discover, "the dwelling in the damp place"! Holding out my hand, I responded to his greeting with something like, "I'm very pleased to meet you, Mr. Bolitho."

To my astonishment he burst into laughter and, adopting a pseudo Cockney accent, replied, "Pleased to meet you, I'm sure!"

My own spirits were surely dampened as I received his suggestion that I was using the lingo of the lower classes and that could only occasion derision. My bitchy if covert response was, "My dear, how far have the colonials come!" It was then I resolved that if my classless Cornishness was to be preserved intact I'd better flee that island as soon as possible and return to the linguistically less restrictive world of North America. Which I did.

# 15
# ALBERTO DE LACERDA

Alberto was another I first met through Derek Patmore. Shortish, dark complexioned with dark field-mousey eyes, he looked wholly Portuguese, even though he was born in Mozambique, where, I think, his father was a colonial administrator. I know next to nothing about his background other than that Stephen Spender implies in his unreliable (see later) *Journals* that he was Jewish — which came as a complete surprise to me. He also refers to Alberto's disillusion with England and Edith Sitwell, whose protégé he was. But again, such was far from the case during the year or more when we were relatively close friends.

Looking back, I now think Alberto was many things to many people — but that is not necessarily to imply duplicity on his part. People often want to perceive a person in such a way as eases themselves or provides them with an excuse or rationale for their own behaviour. Alberto, of course, was indubitably un-English, blue-chinned, excitable, and mischievous, and went about calling himself an artist. He was ever eager to please and avid over social ambition. He was also very free with his sexual advances, and although in my case the incident was brief, mildly embarrassing, and soon forgotten, that wasn't always the case.

The business with me, on the very first time I went to his comfortable ground-floor flat in Chelsea, was as simple as I suspect it was characteristic of his insatiable appetite. I think his motives were mixed, for although he had offered to show me his apartment, we were due to go out again fairly soon as we were to dine afterwards — probably with Derek.

We had but a few minutes of happy chitchat as we peeped into rooms before he reluctantly joined an insistent and neurotically punctual me at the front door. But exit was other than foremost in his mind. I not only felt him push against me in the cramped space of his little hallway but knew immediately afterwards that his cock was ramrod and pressed hard against my bottom.

I was not only set upon our punctual departure but equally set against his rear entry! And that was nothing to do with our arriving late at a restaurant. I wriggled dexterously around, gave his prominence a playful prod, and smilingly informed him that I liked neither to be sodomized nor to play the role of bugger. His charcoal eyebrows rose a centimetre but his smile was as expansive as my own. "Well, we know where we stand, then, don't we," he said (or words to that effect), and the action if not the topic was never raised again between us.

His exploits with at least one other man he told me about somewhat later when we were more relaxed with each other and prone to confessions. His Chelsea address put him in a strategic position to pursue his particular penchant for guardsmen, and it was just outside the barracks of one such battalion that he was discovered and arrested while in the course of anally penetrating a compliant young soldier. Whether money had already passed and prostitution was involved I do not know, but, according to Alberto, before he could be deported, his patron and friend, Edith Sitwell, who, though she spent a lifetime denying that her brother, Osbert, owned similar proclivities, acted boldly and bravely on his behalf. Pulling the kind of strings that national pride suggested begins only on the southern side of the English Channel, the tall and bejewelled minor poetess ensured that Alberto continued to stay in England and continued to translate her poems.

Not that the Sitwells didn't sometimes present problems for the voluble and volatile Alberto. More than once he complained to me (though he was far too proud to borrow the requisite cash) that he had again been invited to the Sitwell family mansion in the Midlands and that he couldn't afford it. I was astonished that the Stately Homes of England could be run on a hotel basis but he quickly corrected that impression by telling me that what he couldn't afford or ignore were the symbolically outstretched hands of the staff of Renishaw Hall – from butler to valet – who lined up for their tips at the departure of the guests at the conclusion of a weekend.

More convenient for our Portuguese poet was an invitation from Dame Edith to the Sesame Club, where she often entertained when in residence in her Hampstead flat. It was on one such occasion that I inadvertently caused Alberto a measure of embarrassment, though we hooted with laughter about it subsequently.

I have earlier in these recollections referred to one Gene Baro, whom I'd met as part of Frank McGregor's entourage in New York City and Kent, Connecticut. Like Alberto, he too had made an unsuccessful pass at me, but it is only now that I am made aware of the coincidence. And in any case, I would be giving an extravagantly false impression if I were to suggest my life has been one of playing hard to get.

Gene arrived in London, at once made contact with me, and because he was staying with an elected member of the London County Council was able to offer me tickets with him to various theatrical and musical venues that had connections with the LCC.

As a result of that, and wishing to repay him with an equal kindness and knowing his appetite for headhunting, I asked Alberto, one day, whether it was at all feasible that Gene could meet the illustrious Dame Edith – or Sir Osbert, her brother, come to that. I may say my request had been rather tentative, as when I had introduced the very minor American poet to the hardly famous Portuguese one they had not appeared to be instantly taken with each other. But here again I must throw in an aside: Floyd and I are notorious at being the opposite of the mythical cupid; more often we have engendered "hate at first sight"!

Whether that was so or not, whether each had discovered an attraction in the other that was hidden from my eyes, Alberto agreed with alacrity to see what he could do. So it was that when I made my first and only entry into the Sesame Club and met Edith Sitwell, it was in the company of the generously proportioned and somewhat flowery Gene Baro. Gene had not come unprepared. He brought his hostess a massive bouquet that evoked from her, so Alberto told me, for I was seated across the table and out of earshot, the observation that she was not a coffin and that she hoped the lunch would not prove funereal.

93

I have long forgotten the precise seating plan but I do recall with reason that the Great Lady was flanked on the one hand by Alberto and on the other by Father Philip Caraman, who was the recent convert to Roman Catholicism's confessor as well as friend. Gene sat next to the elderly priest and was considerably miffed, because not only was he not seated next to the *crème de la crème* herself but he was also well apart from the one or two others there who could lay claim to some literary eminence.

Poor Gene, he was so sophisticated and assured in his own New York lair, not least in the Gramercy Park residence of Frank McGregor, but here in Lit London he was but a baby! Philip Caraman was a priest, as was Father Martin D'Arcy, another Jesuit from their Farm Street church, who was on socially intimate terms with dozens of celebrities — from novelists to movie stars — and on acquaintance would surely have opened as many doors for Gene as he had days to spend in the British capital. Instead Gene treated him as if he were just some transplanted hillbilly cleric who had found himself in the wrong place.

# 16
## STEPHEN SPENDER AND RAYMOND CHANDLER

Of all the people mentioned in these pages there is none over whom I am more ambivalent than Stephen Spender. He is the hardest to write about and discuss because he proved to be the most mendacious predator it has been my misfortune to meet. Yet his impact was one of the most profound.

Although Auden had often mentioned him to me and enlarged upon their shared past, making clear that they were still friends, he did caution me about him in the likelihood I were to encounter him on my return to London. Then Wystan was often bluntly honest about those he knew and never backward in describing them through spectacles of highly critical love.

I'd forgotten all that when I first saw the tallest of Nora Wydenbruck's guests bending his snow-white head over groups of people in her backyard. But as she, too, warned me that the grey-suited poet was prone to be predatory, Wystan's admonitions came flooding back. He was now hovering over the much shorter Alberto de Lacerda — but I was soon to learn that Alberto already had his number and could be as evasive, when needed, as he could be aggressive when erotic roles were switched the other way.

When we met out there in the Holland Park garden things began to move very swiftly between Spender and myself. Too quickly. As it happened, that week I was just about to enter St. Bartholomew's Hospital, where my elder brother had trained, to have an appendectomy. When I came round from the anesthetic it was first to see my Cornish cousin Mary standing there and then — an utter surprise — Stephen Spender alongside her. He proceeded to totally ignore her, my only flesh and blood present, and to launch into an invitation for me to spend my convalescence with his family on Loudon Road in Hampstead.

It would be comfortable to say that it was my weakness after the operation that made me so amenable to his insistence — as it would be to excuse my ignoring of faithful and shy Mary and not remonstrating with him for his rudeness towards her by appearing oblivious of her presence. But my motives can be as mixed as the next and they were on that occasion. The idea of gently healing and resting in the home of a well-known figure, plus the vacation from work at the BBC, had enormous appeal. I hardly hesitated.

For the next ten days or so I was a houseguest at 13 Loudon Road. I naturally met the Spender children, Lizzy and Matthew, and Stephen's peculiar pianist wife, Natasha. I say peculiar advisedly. She was sniffing around the Christian religion at the time and to aid her she had imported a Christian savant from Oxford whose name I unhappily forget. In later times he would have been termed a guru, and he and she carried on a continuous conversation at any meal at which he was present as if they were alone. The only concession to the rest of us would be made by her introducing Jesus into the most mundane conversations. So Natasha would be heard saying, "Oh, there's the phone ringing again, I wonder whether Jesus would answer it." Or in similar vein, "I think Jesus would enjoy that magazine, Stephen — if he could get by that stupid article on truffles."

One day I surprised her in the spacious room where she was playing her Steinway. At the same time she was also listening to an LP of Artur Schnabel, I think. Over the tinkle of Franz Schubert she gaily explained that she always practised in that fashion, as Schnabel's tempi were perfect for that piece of music. She went on to explain that she had a BBC recital in a couple of days and was very nervous about it.

After listening a little longer to the odd duet I made my way over to the large window that looked out onto the Spenders' spacious back garden. I saw a lithe young man at work trimming bushes. He was sunbrowned and stripped naked to the waist.

Natasha must have seen the same for she suddenly stopped playing and switched off Schnabel. "Part of Stephen's unmentionable past," she announced somewhat inconsistently in her rich contralto tremolo.

I should be less than grateful to both Spenders if I failed to record how pleasant they made my stay in their house during my recuperation, for I was in truth feeling physically wan and in need of such caring. As I got stronger Stephen became keen for me to meet his friends. One particular Sunday teatime enabled me to meet a childhood hero, Sir Julian Huxley, the naturalist brother of Aldous, and both the grandsons of the Thomas Huxley, the eminent exponent of Darwin. Unfortunately, his intellectual gifts apart, he proved socially to be egomaniacal, shouting everyone down, including his doormat of a wife. I was shattered to have the idol of my Cornish youth disintegrate into a boor and a bully before my eyes. But at least it meant another illusion gone. The less trust put in kings or princes the better, my biblically minded grandmother would have said.

One London morning Stephen took me to see his friend, the painter Francis Bacon. We entered some ramshackle and, for still frail me, cold premises to find the puffy but boyish-faced man suffering from a severe cold that made a rather adenoidal voice, which characterizes a number of us gays, even more so.

But my most stringent early impressions of this stocky upper-class Irishman (no brogue!) was of the utter squalor in which he both lived and evidently worked. The unmistakable smell of urine made me remark — strictly to myself, I might add — that this was the first time I'd met an artist who pissed and painted in roughly the same place!

The talk was commonplace and consisted mainly of gossip between the two middle-aged gents that flattered me in the assumption I knew who they were talking about but occasionally kindly included me in their references. Bacon was intrigued by my Cornish background. He, as an artist, was familiar with St. Ives. He was much less taken by the fact I was currently a producer for the BBC. It didn't take long to see he was one of those upper-class gays who are fascinated by working-class boys and more than a little cool to what they take as middle-class pretension — an assumption I think the painter made from my brief BBC association.

In other words, yet a further example of the all-pervading notion of class and class division that certainly characterized the British Isles, regardless of sexual gender, in the 1950s — the last period over which I can give personal witness.

The most boring experience I had in that first sustained time with Spender was a visit to a West End cinema to see the biblical epic *The Ten Commandments*. Stephen adored it as he did all such spectacular movies that were currently in vogue. Then I was already growing aware that apart from references to literary personalities, the poet was a stranger to abstraction — indeed, had a minimal mind and was uncomfortable with tough intellectual matters.

Not that such limitations necessarily fettered his indubitable prowess as a minor lyric poet. We were once en route to the Royal Albert Hall, where he was to give a major address at some conference (I now forget what it was in aid of), and he asked me what I thought his best poems were. Without hesitation I said, "The Landscape Near an Aerodrome," and began quoting the opening lines:

> More beautiful than any moth
> With burring furred antennae
> Feeling its huge path

I think he was flattered by that but disappointed that I hadn't come up with something more recent than his work from the early 1930s. But though I was hardly about to tell him, I don't think he ever went beyond such youthful promise. Yet as the most publicized literary figure of his time, one might well be tempted to paraphrase Churchill and say, never in the life of English letters has one person achieved so much prominence on so very little.

Some months later I was back in Paris and again staying at the Presbytère St. Georges as the guest of its chaplain, Father Henry Brandreth. Here Stephen came to visit, filling Henry's guest-hungry heart by inscribing in the visitors' book. Later that day I was visiting some lesbian friends of Derek Patmore, who lived in the vicinity of Stephen's hotel, the Lutetia, I think it was. We shared a cab to that point and both alighted hard by the Chambres des Députés.

He suddenly asked me to his room, just as my appointment with the two American ladies was fast approaching. I politely refused. It was dusk but even had it been broad daylight I don't think it would have stopped him. He grabbed me in a doorway and thrust my hand down towards his already exposed and stiff penis. All I can think is that he felt it was time I paid up for being his guest during my convalescence. In any case, I felt it no time to discuss the matter, what with the gendarmerie always ubiquitous in that vicinity and my next scheduled meeting. I pushed him away hard in the area of the waistcoat of his expensive grey flannel suit and bolted.

The very next time we met was several years later. He was accompanied by Natasha and they came as guests to our apartment facing the Golden Gate Bridge and the island of Alcatraz in San Francisco. He was on a lecture tour and had just performed at Berkeley. After dinner we switched off the main lights and sat on the sofa, looking out at the twinkling magic of the bay. I sat next to Natasha, then Floyd, then Stephen in the opposite corner from me. It was only afterwards that I learned from my lover that Stephen had spent his time not enjoying the nocturnal view but busying himself striving to unzip Floyd's fly. Each time Floyd's hand had firmly removed the alien one, but if persistence was an exam mark Stephen Spender would have graduated in spades! It was then I think I learned that bisexuals, even with their wives in the offing, were far bolder predators than their strictly gay counterparts. It was a lesson confirmed later that year by Emlyn Williams, who fell upon another of our guests — to the latter's acute embarrassment — on the same sofa and with, of course, the same vista of bridge and that grim island prison of Alcatraz in the choppy bay — which, however, failed entirely as a metaphor of warning!

The final incident with the voracious bisexual poet was in our home in Vancouver — or rather in a restaurant where I had been invited to join Spender and a local writer for whom it was palpably evident he had immediately developed the hots. This would have been some twenty years after the San Francisco encounter — not really long enough for the descent of total amnesia on any of the participants. Then I think Stephen's distancing himself from me — ducking innocent questions about his family and brusquely dedicating his *Love Hate Relations* "Stephen Spender for David," when earlier he had inscribed both his *Collected Poems* and his short story volume *The Burning Cactus* identically with "To David with love from Stephen" — had as much to do with his fleshly appetites while in British Columbia as any kind of memory loss.

Corroborative of all that is the nonsense he writes towards the end of his *Journals 1939–1983*, which hardly inspires confidence in what goes before. I quote:

> Few sensations can be more mutually disagreeable than re-meeting former friends after twenty-five years and I daresay Y felt the same. From what he said (and he made numerous over-the-head-of-the-others references to this) we must have met in Berkeley. His voice booms and he pontificates. He talked across the others at me. "I agreed with you so much, Stephen, when we last met at Berkeley and Natasha was there — and Matthew — how is Matthew by the way? — and you said ..."
>
> There was nothing really to be done. Y stroked and stroked and stroked with all his fingers every hair of his beard. Nothing is more lascivious than long fingers combing up and down and in and out of a gingery beard. Bringhurst, who also has a beard — but quite a short one — abstained from touching his, which I took to be a kind of message that he understood my exasperation.

When Spender published that I did not deign to reply — largely, I confess, at Floyd's insistence. But now I want to say that I have never grown a beard (with or without ginger), have stubby fingers, and mentioned his wife and children solely because politeness necessitated it. That it was quite obvious to me that he was hungry for the poet Robert Bringhurst, even though the man appeared straight and utterly unaware of predatory antics.

Perhaps I should add that he was rather cross at a subsequent meeting that evening when I asked him to clarify the business of the CIA's involvement with the magazine *Encounter*, of which he was the literary editor while Irving Kristol, an American, was the political one. The magazine paid far more than any of its peers in London and made no attempt to hide its Anglo-American background. Nevertheless, when it transpired that it had been actually funded by the Central Intelligence Agency as part of the Cold War there was a lot of Brit chagrin — not to say embarrassment. It now seems to me that Stephen subsequently felt he had been played for a sucker.

I present two more encounters under the Spender umbrella to ensure I don't end on a wholly negative note.

It was as editor of *Encounter* that he asked me to contribute a brief "Comment" in response to an article on juvenile delinquency. I did so, centring my piece on middle-aged delinquency. Stephen was helpful in my writing the article — even as he had been earlier over my fiction, stressing that I listen carefully to how people speak to one another and thus learn to differentiate with the talk of my characters. That was a lesson that has stood me in good stead for the remainder of my writing life.

Martha Gellhorn, the ex of Hemingway and now married to Tom Matthews, a retired editor of *Time* magazine, happened to catch my article and wrote to me in Cornwall expressing the wish to meet me if I were ever in London. Needless to say, after the weekend with my parents and my return to Ladbroke Grove I called her and accepted an invitation to have drinks with them. She proved a fascinating woman, and the cocktail party, consisting mainly of well-heeled Americans living in Mayfair and thereabouts, was a lively affair and a complete revelation to me that so many U.S. executives and others lived with their spouses in mid-1950s London. I felt I was back in New York.

Her sixtyish husband was a less happy experience. Deeply disgruntled, a WASP and an anglophobe, he preserved his deepest distaste for queers. My knowledge of this came about in a rather odd fashion. Tom Matthews was to subsequently produce a memoir of T.S. Eliot called *Great Tom*. It is alleged to be full of inaccuracies but as my acquaintanceship with the poet lasted less than a day I can hardly attest to that. But when Matthews discovered that I knew Eliot's place of worship, occasionally attended there myself, and in any case was also an Anglo-Catholic, he zeroed in. "I am a great admirer of Mr. Eliot. He is the greatest poet of the twentieth century, no doubt about it." A slight pause was followed by a quizzical look that wasn't exactly amiable. "Where do you usually go to Mass here on Sundays, then?" He didn't just ask, he barked the question. I thought his father should have been a general rather than a bishop.

"I go to All Saints, Margaret Street, St. Cypriot's, Clarence Gate, where Eliot is a sidesman, I believe, and All Saints Notting Hill, which is closest to where I live. And, of course, St. Mary's Bourne Street."

It was obviously the last he had been waiting for. "That's where all the fairies go, of course. God! Trust my wife to find another!"

"She found me in the pages of *Encounter*," I said acidly.

"And we all know who edits that, don't we?" he leered.

From which I gathered he and Stephen were not friends. Perhaps in the back of my mind I'd been hoping that this man and I might become such. At least to the degree that back in New York I might check out job possibilities with *Time* given his own editorial background as Martha had informed me. But not only his anti-gay attitude but his whole rancorous demeanour had decided I wanted nothing whatever to do with this silver-haired, bow-tied length of animosity. It was only the instant charm and unstinted praise for my little article that persuaded me to accept his wife's invitation to dinner at a nearby restaurant in their company. I would have liked to have seen Ms. Gellhorn again and learned of her pioneering adventures as an early woman journalist — but the price of his accompanying presence, to whom she seemed altogether loyal and united, was just too high. But I still have Stephen Spender to thank for that brief glimpse of a fascinating woman.

Another person I have to thank him for — or maybe it was more thanks to Natasha — was the novelist Raymond Chandler (1888–1959). I met him at the Spenders' place during my convalescence, but it culminated in the grandiose surroundings of the Ritz Hotel, where he took me to dinner. That wasn't altogether an altruistic gesture. By the time I met him, Chandler was elderly, recently widowed, and desperately unhappy. He handled that by being cantankerous, but I could always contend with that by being a bit of a curmudgeon myself. You might call our brief encounter a matter of mutual admiration for our refusal to buckle to the other.

Chandler was born in Chicago but was reared in England and educated at Dulwich College. He served in the Canadian Army during the

First World War. In 1924, months after his mother's death, he married Cissy Pascal, who was eighteen years older than he. Cissy died in 1954 and Chandler died five years later at the age of seventy. His novels include *The Big Sleep* (1939) and *The Long Goodbye* (1953).

If I say that Chandler was one of the most unpleasant people I have had the misfortune to encounter, I should say in the same breath that I saw extenuating circumstances from the outset when we met as fellow dinner guests in the Hampstead home of Stephen and Natasha. He was sodden drunk. He was also still in the chill of the recent death of his wife and spiritually a man looking for assurance and guidance. He and Natasha were enthusiasts of the same Oxford shaman, named, I think, John Williams, who was very popular with certain would-be intellectuals during the mid-1950s.

At first he was highly suspicious of me: partly because I was still single at thirty (and therefore sexually suspect); partly because I was working as a BBC producer and therefore an establishment figure (however minor); and partly because, like many figures with a high profile in their profession — in his case, as an extraordinarily successful author whose novels had so often became Hollywood hits — he was profoundly paranoid in the assumption that the world at large was eternally seeking to exploit him.

The broad hostility colouring his initial attitude towards me soon took a more critical turn. So I had been to New York and San Francisco. What the hell did that mean? That I had any true knowledge of the United States? British bullshit if I did!

What did I mean, claiming to be a writer? What the hell had I written? More importantly, what of mine had *he* read? I mentioned my first book, a study in contemporary French Catholicism, not because I thought he would be impressed by a theological tome, however slight in length, scope, and appeal, but because it was the only book I had ever published. He thrust spit-moist lips forward in a sneer but only said, "What else?"

I frantically mentioned a BBC "Talks" script, and an article that was shortly to appear in *Encounter* for which journal Spender was the literary editor. That proved a major mistake. I was still unaware that he was interested in the mind and soul of Natasha Spender and was contemptuously dismissive of her spouse. And being Raymond Chandler, he said as much.

He then proceeded to quiz me about my knowledge of his own novels and stories — and, alas, found me wanting.

I was not one of those growing number of middle- and upper-brow readers (particularly in France and England) who put Chandler in a unique category as an author who could be forgiven vulgar commercial success because of his crispness of style, a remarkably authentic evocation of the terrain and ethos of Southern California, and, indeed, the general superiority of his prose compared to that of most practitioners of the whodunit in those pre–P.D. James times.

However, it was worse than that. Not only was I not an enthusiast of Raymond Chandler's oeuvre but the whole genre was uncongenial to me. Nor did it even stop there. Had I been in conversation with Charles Dickens I would still have had a problem. I have always had a frustratingly weak memory, especially for such data as book titles, symphony numbers, and the names of particular paintings or sculptures. All these factors now combined with an overwhelming amnesia further stimulated by my dislike of the testy old gent whose self-importance he was so concerned to stress there in the Spenders' living room before a doting Natasha. In the space of a few hours I was made vividly aware that the creator of Philip Marlowe was patently the peer of his character when it came to recording facts, paying infinite attention to detail, and demonstrating the power to faithfully recollect it.

What had begun as a general disposition to being prickly soon turned into an antagonism born of mental opposites — supported by a growing anti-English attitude (he had been, I suspect, alternatively snubbed, patronized, and insulted since he had arrived in the vulnerability of widowhood in the British capital) and a latent homophobia the origins of which I didn't start to contemplate.

By the second time we met (I must have been seduced by the prospect of lunch at the Savoy, as by the time of my departure from the Spender home that evening I had taken a firm dislike to the sour little man), he was, albeit minusculely, more pleasant.

We did not take up where we had left off at the dinner party studiously avoiding each other in conversation. Instead we both elected neutral territory.

I asked him about John Williams, his Oxford guru, and he started to quiz me about my London life, who I knew in local literary circles, and what was my family background. Only I don't wish to give the impression that it was a give-and-take conversation as we sat over oysters followed by cold pheasant (his choices) during the Savoy luncheon. He told me he was growing restless with the excessively hothouse atmosphere he had found at Oxford, virtually ignored my question about the spiritual teachings of Williams, and from then on proceeded to deliver a steady monologue over bloodsucking bastards in Los Angeles, the treachery of friends, his overall loneliness, and the need for understanding. All this lasted well through the meal and was steadily punctuated by the quaffing of Scotch and an occasional glass of the excellent Moët & Chandon champagne he had generously ordered on my behalf.

It was then a strange thing happened. Indeed, the very thing that prompts me to include Raymond Chandler in this gallery of cameo portraits of people I have known to greater or lesser degree.

When he exhausted his list of people he would never forgive, never again trust, and who had proved such despicable beings when he had sought comfort on his wife's death, he turned to the future. His rather dry, metallic voice (that fluctuated more in volume than tone) was accompanied by the occasional stab of a delicate, well-manicured finger protruding from a rather effeminately small hand. He claimed ignorance of Continental Europe — and interrupted his soliloquy momentarily to ask me whether I knew France, Spain, and Italy at all.

When I answered rather immodestly in the affirmative, he outlined a plan to wander from place to place, down through France to the Mediterranean, and then tackle Italy, followed by the Iberian Peninsula, in which he mentioned the Balearic Islands as well as the rest of Spain, then Portugal and finally back to France via Biarritz.

As he spoke, he seemed to me as I grew mildly woozy from the champagne actually to change shape. His body appeared to shrink as his head grew larger, wobbling progressively while his voice took on something really approaching a whine. So emphatic did the latter become that I forced myself from reverie over his physical transformation and listened more carefully to what he was saying. That first proved fascinating, then alarming.

He told me that he had come back to England from California because he found life, now that his wife, faithful companion for so many years, was gone, had become unbearable because of the pain of memories. He said that England, in the few weeks he'd been there, had also become a nightmare, as he had built up so many illusions about the place of his upbringing and education at Dulwich College, which had proved to be a nest of rapacious bloodsuckers — a favourite term of his — in its whining supplication for his money for an endowment.

He thought that civilized France and the warmth and balm of the Mediterranean lands might give him sustenance. He then told me that he was dying.

My champagne lost its bubbles, and whatever was on my plate became inedible. There was nothing I could think to say; I just waited for him to continue — which he did without much of a pause. He had known it before he had left California, indeed the chief reason for his going to Oxford and seeking spiritual advice from that spiritual fake, Williams, was his awareness of his approaching demise. He did not specify the nature of his illness but continued to elaborate his plans for what future he had left.

He did hint, however, that whatever his illness was it would lead to progressive disability and that he could not contemplate travelling around Europe without a companion of some kind. Someone to arrange scheduling, hotel bookings, restaurants, and the like.

Then he switched abruptly to the personal: to me, that is.

"I know you must get a pretty good salary from the BBC, but I would pay you a whole lot more. You could call your own price, in fact."

I wanted to stop him, but I didn't know how. I had never talked to someone who knew they were dying and had but a short time to live. Nor had I ever been propositioned for a job in the Savoy Hotel, London.

He babbled on. "I don't expect you to have medical knowledge, of course. We could always hire someone else for that when it proves necessary. We would work out a proper routine, hours, time off and all that. I am a man of routine, you see, David. I like it all laid out in detail. Fair pay for a fair day's work. That's the ethic I grew up on."

They are not his exact words. Tape recorders were in their infancy — besides, I didn't own one. But the gist is right. He continued in a similar vein. Outlining for me a daily program to which he had obviously already devoted time and which evoked for me an all-encompassing image of an amanuensis, personal companion, and male nurse.

Whatever the emphases he adumbrated over the various overlapping roles, whatever the stress he gave the financial rewards and the laxity of control, I still found the whole thing personally abhorrent. But I was just thirty and an immature thirty at that. Instead of a succinct "no," I launched into a personal catalogue of reasons why such a position was utterly alien to my future plans and that my disposition radically opposed being at the beck and call of anyone — let alone a personal employer. In short, that I was not cut out to be a gentleman's companion. The trouble was that I didn't tell him that in short. I went on and on — was as drearily prolix as my host.

With the perception of afterthought — and maybe a small degree of wisdom brought by the ensuing years — I think my opposition to his surprising plans was not only fuelled by my delight in my current job at the BBC and the long-term arrangement to rejoin my California lover as soon as financially possible, but out of a deep-rooted suspicion that he had dreamed up this role for me from his stereotypical belief in the homosexual character who would be happiest serving a straight male in the positions he had so carefully outlined. After all, didn't gays make good waiters, and were not many of them male nurses and companions and even gentlemen's gentlemen?

That arrogant generalization — along the lines that "black Americans have rhythm" or "Asian faces are hard to read" — was enough then as it is now to make me want to upchuck. And in less than gentle language I told him so.

The end of that lunch was as frosty as the dinner that had preceded it, and I never saw him again. However, that was 1955 and Raymond Chandler did not die until four years later — after he had in fact long since returned to California.

It wasn't altogether a negative experience, though. I have something to thank him for. When we first sat down in the Savoy, he gave me a package, which he imperiously insisted I not open then and there. In fact, it wasn't until I sat atop the bus heading west down the Strand that I did so.

It proved something of a surprise. It wasn't one of his own books, which I might more or less have expected, but a copy of the novel *The Night of the Hunter* by Davis Grubb. I still have it. On the flyleaf is inscribed the following: "Raymond Chandler, Box 128, La Jolla, California, May 5, 1954."

I started reading and almost forgot my bus stop I was so captivated. I not only thoroughly enjoyed the highly melodramatic work of the unwarrantedly obscure Ohio River author but also subsequently loved its cinematic offspring, which turned out to be my favourite movie, *The Night of the Hunter* (1955), directed by Charles Laughton and starring Robert Mitchum, Shelley Winters, and Lillian Gish.

# 17
# DAVID HUGHES AND ROY JENKINS

I met the youthful biographer of J.B. Priestley and later novelist David Hughes when I was at the BBC and we both lived in Bayswater. He worked when I first knew him for John Lehman, who was editing *London Magazine* and who happened to do a broadcast for me during the same period. Then subsequently David worked for Paul Elek, the publisher-adventurer.

David was a fresh and lively figure, recently down from Oxford, son of a schoolmaster and a devotee of both contemporary writing and attractive young women. We had the *former* in common. He endeared himself to me quite early on when I think he was pursuing a girl visitor to St. Basil's House, where I was living. He told me that when he had brought the tall and rather gloomy Lehman (he always reminded me personally of a well-groomed raptor) to his father's Wimbledon house the latter, a headmaster, was singularly unimpressed. In due course, their guest had to pee, and David, on hearing the loud splash of their guest's falling water coming from the hall toilet, exclaimed to his still impervious father, "Do you realize, Dad, how privileged we are to be listening to the peeing of one of the most famous poets in England?"

David was buoyant in his endless joy and optimism. I can't make any generalization, pompous or otherwise, about his position in mid-1950s Britain, as he was a whole new species to me. Younger by four years, he already had a successful Oxford career under his belt and more than his big toe now in the London publishing world. He was to write several successful novels, be a high-profile literary journalist, and in 1985 win the W.H. Smith Literary Award. Twice married and father of two children, his first wife was the Swedish actress Mai Zetterling, with whom, I recall, he lived in a charming rural ex-vicarage.

He helped me tackle a first biography of D.H. Lawrence, which proved a failure until I rewrote it many years later as a major documentary for the Canadian Broadcasting Corporation. He also found me paid work as a ghost author of an autobiography of an Englishman in the French Foreign Legion and that also proved a disaster — part from my own ineptitude, but also because the subject turned out to be a liar of such proportions that egregious as its adjective would be an understatement.

David, bright, worldly-wise, and sharing my rather juvenile sense of humour (we would write each other cheques for millions of pounds!), was nevertheless possessed of an innocence that I have always found irresistible in people. I think it is akin to the "holy fool" as evoked by the Russian Fyodor Dostoevsky. Anyway, in sickness and health, in disappointment and triumph — and David Hughes drank deep at all those troughs — he  retained a purity of spirit that I have tried, albeit unsuccessfully, to emulate.

We last saw him in 1992 when we invited him to lunch at the Ivy in London. I had brought him a copy of my then new novel, *Thy Mother's Glass*. It was the first time he had ever met Floyd and years since I'd seen him. He had forgotten to bring his own new book and had had to dart into a second-hand bookstore in Charing Cross Road. There he discovered a Penguin copy of his novel, *The Pork Butcher* (subsequently filmed as *Souvenir* with Christopher Plummer and Catherine Hicks), which he inscribed to the two of us as follows: "For David & Floyd, with love from David, on an occasion decades late."

That lunch between three late-middle-aged gents was blissful. Then, though sadness lurked at his gates, I still considered David my life's blithe spirit.

I never really took my job with the BBC's *Third Programme* seriously — partly, in fact, because I thought daily, even hourly, of rejoining my Floyd now back in California, and partly because I was the inveterate outsider in that world of lofty high purpose, laced with imported Continental earnestness and English suavity. I think one story will serve to illustrate what I mean. My boss (nemesis?) P.H. Newby asked me, for my first assignment, if I could find a suitable reviewer for a new book by an Anglican priest named D. Sherwin Bailey. The book's title was *Homosexuality and the Western Christian Tradition*. I think that the reason it became my initial task at Broadcasting House tells you something of Howard Newby's perception of me from the outset. In any event it was never, at least in my hearing, ever referred to again by its title by either Newby or anyone else at the BBC. It was only alluded to as "Sherwin Bailey's Book."

In similar vein, when I told Newby that I thought the current dean of Sidney Sussex College, Cambridge, an Anglican priest with a Freudian background, might be an apt reviewer he seemed only vaguely interested. But when I added that my friend from Paris days, Dr. Robert Casey, was an American, he was all enthusiasm. He explained, "When you're dealing with a prickly subject like this, the Yanks are best. Our listeners can't pigeonhole American voices and therefore don't get so upset."

It was towards the end of my BBC career that I met someone else who I decided was also impossible to pigeonhole — even though he was a Welshman, the son of a coalminer, and a Labour MP. I was returning by train from Birmingham and our BBC studios there. In spite of my first-class ticket, as all BBC producers had, there seemed to be no spare places in the first-class dining car. A distinct and well-modulated voice suddenly boomed an invitation to join him at his table. It was Roy Jenkins, on his way back to London — we shared residences in Notting Hill, in fact — from his parliamentary constituency in the Midlands.

He did most of the talking. Then this was after Stephen Spender had advised me to become a first-rate listener if I intended to end up a first-rate writer — and besides, as a *Third Programme* "Talks" producer, I was also always looking for potential broadcasters. In any case, he was a fascinating speaker and I was entranced as I ate unappetizing British Rail food and heard what he had to say. Starting with the fact that although he respected his constituents he found them an exhausting bunch and he was glad he didn't have to visit his local offices too often! I took time to wonder what they, in turn, must have thought of this well-dressed chap who spoke as if he were more familiar with a silver spoon than the coal pick of his old man.

He was the first MP I'd met who really articulated a love for the fact of Parliament that went beyond party loyalties and the parochial limitations of a particular time in history. In no way did I consider him a diluted Labourite or one about to break ranks. But when he spoke of parliamentary personalities it was free of party restriction and bias. I was not surprised when, so very many years later, he produced his excellent book on Winston Churchill.

He stressed the "club" factor of the House of Commons — but, again, not in the stuffy sense of the London clubs for the various elite but a place where people truly shared and where tradition was not an oppression but a reassuring springboard for originality of thought.

Up to that chance meeting on a speeding train I had not given much thought to what was or wasn't a *statesman*. When we alighted at Euston station and he introduced me to his wife, who drove us all back to Notting Hill, I realized that I had been in the presence of one since leaving Birmingham.

David Watmough, past president of the Federation of University Conservative Associations, a member of the Vermin Club (after Aneurin Bevan referred to the middle class as "vermin"), ended up regarding a Labour minister of the Crown as the politician he most admired in the England he was about to leave permanently.

# 18
# WILL READY

What do you get from a Welsh-born Irishman who served in the British Army, married a woman from the Canadian Prairies, and now fetched up as the acquisitions librarian at Stanford University in California? You get Will Ready, mighty reader, of encyclopedic memory (especially of book titles and that war he fought in), novelist, night owl, heavy drinker, and father of four — or was it five?

It was in my earliest days in California that I met the stocky gent from Cardiff and his tall wife, for they became my landlords in the large house at the edge of the Stanford golf course in whose clubhouse I ate my first hamburger and my first BLT and drank my first (and last) glass of iced tea.

Although he had kindly offered me a room in his home and seemed to find my company sufficiently congenial night after night, a rather rocky scenario took place just out of earshot (for he never mentioned the subject) and out of eyeshot, too, until I received a letter from a Bishop Stephen Neill, who was serving on the World Council of Churches in Geneva. The letter was an anxious inquiry as to my sex life and the fear that I was already steeped in sin, so soon after taking up permanent residence in the U.S. of A. All this because my host and his wife had heard unwonted noises coming from the bedroom adjacent to their own (mine!) when Floyd came back for a weekend leave from his U.S. Army base at Ford Ord where he was doing his military training.

I guess we had expressed our joy and affection at being reunited in a rather noisy way on our shared bed through the small hours of the night.

As it happened, I knew quite a bit about this Bishop Stephen Neill, even though we had never met. He had heard of my misdoings via my Roman Catholic librarian landlord, who had in turn informed Rab Minto, the Scottish Presbyterian minister who was the Stanford University chaplain. Rab had then taken upon himself to contact his friend, the Anglican bishop, whom he knew had read my book, *A Church Renascent*, because *his* friend, the dean of King's College, had furnished the enthusiastic preface. So goes the ecumenical Christian network when excited by real sin such as two young male lovers enjoying sex together!

More at the level of gossip was my own information about the solicitous bishop. When I was still a student at King's I became firm friends (and have remained so to this day) with a young priest who in fact fulfilled the role of tutor for me even though the college didn't use the traditional tutorial system. Harold both taught Greek and was in charge of the music at King's. Now as it happened, his uncle was a minister in the newly constituted Church of South India at the same time that Stephen Neill was. Harold had received a letter from his uncle that mentioned that the bishop had been found disciplining students with an excess that suggested erotic appetite. After a second or perhaps third occasion it had been quietly suggested to his Lordship that possibly India and its young men were spiritually corrupting him and that he might be better back in Europe. Although I imagine it was his undoubted brilliance as a scholar that led him to the World Council of Churches job in Switzerland.

I wrote Stephen Neill, telling him that I didn't feel in need of counsel over the person I gave thanks to God daily for having entered my life. If he were alive today I would be able to write and tell him that I was still offering the same thanksgiving for Floyd well over fifty years later.

Oddly enough, Will Ready's apparent concern over my deviancy had nothing to do with the enthusiastic range of his reading, which certainly included early gay novels such as *Look Down in Mercy* (although that did have a military setting too), the early works of Angus Wilson, and Mary Renault's novels such as *The Charioteer*, which he also wholeheartedly admired.

I think Will was the first person I met whose literary tastes were unencumbered by biases of baggage over gender or the like. It was the likes of him that sparked in me the resolve to be equally objective — not least

114

when confronting a novel or story or play whose political affinities were alien from my own. He also prepared me to view with scornful dismissal the later opponents of voice appropriation who have tried to squeeze writers into suffocating boxes of their own race and gender.

About my time with Will Ready there hangs the ghostly presence of his wife, made gaunt by childbirth — in my days there at Stanford she was forever pregnant — with her numerous children clinging at her skirts as she bent over the sink or wearily ironed.

There was something intriguing about two of the little Ready boys. One was Liam, the other, I think, Sean. Both of them, like their father, had the suspicion of leprechaun ears, so that at the tops they came almost to a point. That characteristic was to lead to a rather startling identification more than forty years later and a thousand miles north in Vancouver. I include it here because it is a somewhat dramatic illustration of how one's life is a much more whole, homogenous thing than one often suspects. At least, that is to say, mine has certainly been.

Perhaps I should start by recording an incident at Stanford, when I'd first moved in with the Readys. I was entering a room on campus — I have forgotten the when and why of it — when a person standing nearby suddenly asked me whether I was David Watmough. When I said yes he merely nodded, and I asked him where we had met.

"At Coopers'," he replied. "You were in the fourth form and I was only in the third. But no one came through a doorway like you did. You just did it again and I knew at once who it was." But when I tried to get him to describe exactly what was the Watmuffian style of entering a room he couldn't really tell me. To my great frustration, I still don't know.

My own means of recognizing this particular person was far more facile. It was at the wake for a pioneer art gallery owner and later curator of the university art gallery, Alvin Balkind, a contemporary who had served in the U.S. Navy when I had been doing likewise in the Royal Navy. His life partner, architecture professor Abe Rogatnik, had asked me to say a few words about my friend, the deceased. When standing there in the crowded foyer I noticed a tall bearded young man staring intently at me. When I had finished he approached me and said, "You won't know who I am."

"To the contrary," I replied. "You are Liam Ready, the son of Will Ready." I had recognized those telltale ears! I swear the only confusion I could have possibly made would have been with his pointy-eared brother. Not that I alluded to the ears per se, fearing it might sound rude, but merely said he had inherited the incredibly distinctive facial features of his father.

His astonishment settled, he filled me in on the years since I had last set eyes on him and his dad. Will had quit Stanford and come to Canada — possibly at his wife's instigation and yearning to return to her native land — though I had never seen her in anything but a sadly slavish role in those early days for me in California.

He became the librarian at McMaster University in Hamilton, Ontario, where, during another illustrious career, he acquired for the university the important papers of the philosopher Bertrand Russell. When I was told that the triple irony wasn't lost on me: the Roman Catholic librarian (whatever the degree of lapse there might be) had secured the major documentation of a lifelong atheist and free thinker and thus brought library lustre to an institution that had its genesis amid ardent Baptists!

Will, I was told, had retired and died in Victoria, enjoying his booze to late in life. His wife was still there as a widow; the other children were scattered but successful in their various enterprises.

# 19

# WALLACE STEGNER
# AND DALE GRAFF

When I started monitoring Iowa-born Wallace Stegner's creative writing classes at Stanford, I was immediately reminded of something I'd read in the pages of George Orwell. This quiet-voiced, blond-looking man personified the quality that the English writer called "decency." He was also one of the very few Americans I have met who had an intuitive and creative awareness of the Canadian fact and its subtle, if elusive, existence under the cultural North American umbrella provided by the United States.

That significance became more personal for me at a latter date, but right off the bat I sensed the virtue of this man's quiet prose and storytelling skills. I needed that before I could get over an innate skepticism of all creative writing departments and the implication that the literary arts can be taught like any other subject. That hesitation on my part has been subsequently modified — I even "taught" creative writing for the Okanagan Summer School of the Arts for many years in the 1960s and 1970s. But nevertheless, a residuum of hesitation remains to this day. Better be a thoroughly experienced and reasonably successful author in the first place, and with an instinct for apprentices in the manner of some painters and sculptors.

With Stegner it was always one-on-one and that, too, is a vital key to the whole creative writing business. I cannot say "He taught me this or that" or even that "this aspect of his own writing rubbed off and that didn't," but he instilled in me a confidence and an assurance that I was on the right track with my still rather juvenile scrawlings, and I cannot thank him enough for that.

Stegner, the author, is essentially the regionalist – the whole North American west, from Saskatchewan down to Utah, including California, being his literary parish. It was that I sensed and I avidly seized on it, for, in spite of my Cornish uprooting and subsequent travels, I was already thirsting to put down writerly roots. In the event, I had to wait for the fertile literary soil of British Columbia to do just that but the yeast of the likes of Wallace Stegner was already doing its work.

There was another factor that attracted me to this author, although, in fact, it had nothing whatever to do with writing per se. Stegner was born in small-town (Lake Mills) Iowa, and Floyd's family is also from rural sections (Clarion) of the same state. With my own agricultural background and doubtless romantic propensity, I saw a linkage between the three of us and found it easy to believe that destiny had had a hand in placing me on the same campus at that particular time with these two excellent Americans!

I shouldn't leave the subject of Stegner without making specific allusion to his fiction, which I think is some of the most powerful I have had the fortune to read. I say this because I still think he is an underestimated author, and who knows, perhaps I have the gall to place myself in that same basket!

His *Collected Stories* are themselves memorable but I reserve a specially subjective love for *Crossing to Safety* for its treatment of profound friendship as I've experienced, *The Spectator Bird* for doing likewise with that old age that I now know, and *Recapitulation* for being one of several inspirations for my own novel *The Moor Is Dark Beneath the Moon* because of its exploration of a man who returns to another place for the funeral of his aunt but confronts his own past instead.

Some writers wear a persona quite at variance with their prose; not so Wallace Stegner. Of course there is the necessary distinction between the storyteller and his tale but I don't think I'm being overly imaginative when I read and reread his fiction and at once recall the measured tones, the twinkling eyes and lined countenance, and the relaxed disposition of the true Westerner. This was a man of real intellectual clout and profound

insight into the human condition who could perhaps give the unpercep-
tive the impression of a rather sluggish man in love with the good life,
dazzled and deadened by the California sun. Ever see a basking lizard
move into lightning action? That was Stegner.

It was in those very early days at Stanford, when I worked as an assistant
in the library and felt rather lonely as an outsider who was not really part
of the community, that I met a handful of students and others who lived
in Palo Alto or who visited friends there regularly, coming down from the
city of San Francisco. Among the latter was a young man originally from
St. George, Utah, a "jack" Mormon (i.e., a rejected one) who worked in a
store that sold sophisticated and expensive lamp fittings. To this point I
had only met students or older people secure in their occupations, so this
was a revelation and a stimulating one at that — for Dale Graff proved to
be one of the most singular and talented individuals I have ever met. He
died of AIDS while still relatively young and still thumbing his nose at
every shade of pretension.

First and foremost I must speak of his laconic wit, which seemed to me
as dry as the gullies and rocks of his native Utah. There are so many kinds
of wit, yet people are often as incapable of differentiating between them
as they are unable to distinguish smells and possess only lowly degrees of
taste. My wit, genetically inherited from my mother, is highly contingent
upon speed of reaction to statements made to me; Dale's cool comments
relied on a drawl of response to things and a wry twist employing mockery
that could quickly turn pompous mountains into humble molehills.

I think at first I was a little afraid of Dale, but I find it extremely hard
to provide specific reasons. I'm pretty sure it was more to do with me than
him. After all, I was the newcomer to California, still the would-be novelist
rather than an actual one. Then Floyd has always insisted that in spite of
some appearances to the contrary — i.e., what Spender called my "booming
voice" and plenty of words as backup — I am a shy person, nervous over new
encounters and having embarrassing blackouts over the names and histo-
ries of people that I really know. Certainly book launches, where one has to

remember the purchaser's accurate name and write something germane, are always a potential horror. And press interviews are, again, a bugbear.

Dale, on the other hand, was on his own elected turf there in California, and with his easy assurance, and his slim and invariably neat figure, he was the epitome of what I was not! Later, when I came to know and admire his paintings — mainly still lifes, which meant he was coolly running against the prevailing tide — I found that assurance, that polish that was so far from slick or lightweight. It really spoke of a thoroughly digested idiom that like so much of what he met in life, as a sales assistant of sophisticated goods, and subsequently as a hard-working elementary school teacher in Oakland, mainly of black and other working-class kids, he made utterly and seamlessly his own.

Yet a mystery hung about him. I have referred earlier to his singular talents but throughout his life he was a stranger to high reputation and public acknowledgement of his gifts beyond the small, mainly gay coterie he numbered among his friends. But for his painting alone I always thought he deserved a defining status, let alone for his unerring artistic eye, his sense of proportion over all things, and, of course, that graceful wit that enriched every gesture and thought. His family background was Swiss and I sometimes thought that there was something of Swiss impeccability in his personality. But even as I write that I am once again aware that it is not through pedigree that I shall find a key to what mystifies me about him. Indeed, I now accept the fact that I shall never know the answer to why such as he travel through life, known only to friends and familiars, and others break into realms of fame and fortune without an iota more talents or benisons.

Not only Dale, but others, too, I have met — writers, composers, singers, painters, the list doesn't stop — who appear to my critical eye and acumen every bit the peer of others who are today household names and have their works proclaimed worldwide. The easy way out is to evoke luck, the will to succeed, and just plain old flukes. Accepting such as profound realities, I myself am prone to fall back on the Greek certainties. They would cite the likes of destiny and fate — and invoke the germane deities to explain triumph and failure.

The Hellenistic gods apart, I do believe that beyond inner conviction and the willingness to sacrifice — and granted everything else being equal — there remains a deep and perhaps unsolvable mystery over why, as the parable in the First Gospel says, "many are called but few chosen." To push the biblical metaphor further, the whole thing still leaves me in "outer darkness," and when I think of Dale, and his peers met along the way, I am tempted "to weep and gnash my teeth." Then one of the things you learn through loving your friends is that in all affection there is mystery. Through those who perhaps never did get an inkling of the recognition they so rightly deserved, there might also be learned a simple lesson of gratitude.

# 20
# JEAN ARTHUR

If I claimed to know Jean Arthur in any accepted sense of that word I should be lying. But nevertheless, when at thirty-two I was just half her age, I met her, spent time with her, broke rice if not bread with her, and found time to marvel at the gap between a screen image and this shy woman I ended up dining with in a San Francisco Chinese restaurant.

There was a palpable connection between the private and public icons. Just as on the screen, there were the brown eyes, the husky (oh so husky!) voice, and the delicate and petite body. But there the semblances stopped.

No openly lesbian presences on the screen, of course. "Remember the era," I was about to write — until realizing that little or nothing has changed for the lesbian image between the 1959–60 of which I write and the present. Dykes are still not dominant features on our large or small screens. Nor have they garnered a serious respect as, in substantial degree, the gay male world has achieved. Their important time is still to come.

So I was not prepared for the firm if quiet way Ms. Arthur handled things. Dare I say *masterly?*

Let me first set the scene. My lover and I had rendezvoused in a Portuguese Sapphist's record store on the Monterey Peninsula when we were visiting relatives in Pacific Grove. Through her we had met her close friend, Jean Arthur, and it was arranged that we three would meet for a second time when the actress came up next to San Francisco. She always stayed at the Mark Hopkins on Nob Hill, as the management there was hospitable to her dogs.

But we arranged to meet not at the hotel but at a Chinese restaurant in the vicinity (Chinatown is but a few blocks away), where Miss Arthur would be in the company of her guru. There we would be joined by further mutual friends and in fact we turned out to be a party of eight, I think — which was a natural boon to selection when eating Chinese food.

It has been my experience that many movie stars living in the Los Angeles area found the relative remoteness and relaxedness of San Francisco a distinct relief. This was particularly true of heterosexuals who kept their mistresses there and gays who just felt easier with the San Francisco bar scene and even gay social life — Rock Hudson being a case in point.

So it was no surprise to find the lesbian Miss Arthur relaxed, even scintillating, in the all-male company in the Chinatown restaurant. Her brown eyes danced mischievously and although I had to strain at times to hear her — she was seated next to me but the gravelly voice was low and quiet — she had witty observations to make and, contrary to things I'd heard, did not seem at all put out on learning that I was a neophyte feature writer with the *San Francisco Examiner*.

Then arrived the mountains of food ordered by the distinguished-looking Chinese gent to her right. He had straight hair, pulled back tight to the nape of his neck, greying sideburns, and a straggly moustache that merged with a wispy beard that, in my movie-oriented and English-parochial mind, I thought belonged only to Mandarins or the Swedish-born Warner Oland period travesty of a Chinese man as Dr. Fu Manchu.

It was Jean Arthur's guru rather than the film star herself who was the dominant at our assembly, and I'm sure that was very much what she wished. But the reason was less to do with personality than dexterity. He had the precision of a heron when it came to stabbing things with his chopsticks. And here I must digress.

When I moved first from San Francisco to Vancouver it was to find a town where muffins and marmalade were considered exotic and dim sum unheard of. But that was the late 1950s and things were beginning to change — rapidly. Living in a North American city with the most established Chinatown outside Asia and where the Chinese and Japanese factors were both integrated and substantial, I had every opportunity to embrace the chopstick. But I mulishly stuck with the feudal fork. Today I am shamed by usually being the only one needing the Western weapon when sitting with my friends, confronting tempura or teriyaki in a Japanese restaurant, or egg rolls and deep-fried shrimp in a Chinese one. Indeed, I have attended one of the now scores of Japanese restaurants and cafés for lunch in Vancouver and watched Caucasian artisans discussing their jobs, say, on a nearby housing complex, as they dexterously tackle their rice with similar ease to that demonstrated by Jean Arthur's friend those many years ago.

Only his was on shrimp, which I adored. And seemingly just a split second before I (having decided on a succulent lump of crustecea) was about to pounce, he had him in a flash, forestalling and frustrating my slower-moving fork with his unerring sticks.

It would be nice to record scintillating conversation, but if there was any it went over my head. We talked dogs a little bit. Mainly hers, that was, for we did not secure our first, the gentle basset hound, Wendy, until we moved briefly to New Jersey and then took her with us when we settled in Vancouver.

Movies and Hollywood were taboo subjects at her request and most of the talk was of Carmel and the Monterey Peninsula for which we were all greater or lesser enthusiasts. With the exception of her guru, that is. Then he was so busy spearing and eating that he had hardly time for superficial chit-chat.

Even without animated talk or the exchange of profound or merely professional insights, my one and only encounter with a movie star was an educative experience. And that arose out of my immediate awareness of how truly vulnerable a human being she was, with the implication that whether one is immersed in fame — or bereft of it — makes no difference if one has inherited a deep shyness and an instinct for the quiet and the dark. This still remains so, even if destiny has led to the spotlight and the drums of publicity.

As they stabbed and I pronged, and Jean spoke lovingly of her elderly mother and her sheltered and private headland home on the edge of Carmel, I reflected on others who were perhaps similar to my famous neighbour at the circular table: Greta Garbo, for instance. Or the painful dilemmas of a shy monarch like George VI or his daughter, Queen Elizabeth II — both of whom were prepared to suffer the antithesis of their natures in the cause of duty. Something that we lesser mortals are prepared to do, but often only for the sake of livelihood.

I think shyness was an agony for Jean Arthur, perhaps more so than her sexual propensities. But somehow she had successfully knit these challenges with other elements in her personality kit and the result was that the rather petite figure sitting next to me, all else said, remained a glamorous and radiant film star.

# 21

# NIVEN BUSCH
# (AND HIS KIND)

If I were not to meet another Hollywood luminary of the likes of Jean Arthur, I was to meet the ghost of one, as well as some of the cohort of important names in the movie industry who, in that weird and wonderful world of Southern California, often yield more clout than the stars. Then, for those that don't know it, there are two distinct Californias — more apart in some ways than, say, Ireland and England.

An encounter when I was a features writer with the *San Francisco Examiner* illustrates my point. My perverse but brilliant boss, Bill Hall, had designed a crash course for my Americanization. Knowing that I was "fresh off the boat," he liked to provide assignments that would test and hone my journalistic skills by centring on subjects of which I knew nothing.

In short term I was given a series on western rodeos, on California counties, on baseball (the Giants having newly arrived at Candlestick Park, south of the city), and, as a long-term venture, on movie personalities and projects.

It was in the latter context I met Henry Ephron and Jean Negulesco, both of whom were involved in the writing and direction of the film adaptation of Françoise Sagan's *A Certain Smile* when they came to San Francisco to boost their product.

I was dined at one of San Francisco's finest restaurants (my choice) and much of the vacuous talk was about their highly "intellectual" and "artsy" film, for which San Francisco, widely known for both properties, would be the ideal site for the initial opening. Could I provide them with the name of a specific movie house suitable as a first-run house to judge audience reaction? I couldn't, so they would investigate personally and get back to their studio's research department.

Whether it was the doing of the two visiting gents or their Los Angeles backup, *A Certain Smile* had its preview in Oakland, of all places — presumably to an audience of sailors and blue-collar workers. That at least brought *a certain smile* to the faces of my *Examiner* colleagues — the East Bay community not being regarded as the intellectual hub of the Bay Area, let alone as the haven for connoisseurs of sophisticated movies.

Another encounter while employed by the *Examiner* was with author Niven Busch, who wrote the novel *Duel in the Sun* and the screenplay for *The Postman Always Rings Twice*, plus many other movie scripts. He had been married to Teresa Wright of *Mrs. Miniver* fame. Along with Tom King, the *Examiner* photographer, and still to this day a close friend, I had an extraordinary dinner with the Busches on their secluded ranch near Tres Pinos in San Benito County (it was when I was involved in my California county series for the paper's weekend magazine), about nine miles out of Hollister.

Although now married to Carmencita, Niven's two offspring from Teresa Wright hung like taut little ghosts about the dinner proceedings. Then maybe her own matriarchal Mrs. Miniver spirit lingered there in the slightly self-consciously civilized setting of the ranch.

Carmencita was herself what might be described as a Mexican Californian aristocrat, coming as she did from those ruling Mexicans who reluctantly yielded their power to the United States when it took over the state. However, that didn't prevent her from acting the bitch when she was prevailed upon to go to town and return with dinner. She insisted on speaking Spanish, which was native to none of us, and generally behaving as if we had emerged from a lower life to see her husband. I understand she later married a cowboy and I think she might well have been happier lording it over a more tractable social inferior. For most of the evening she spoke of her childhood and youth in San Francisco where, I think, her family owned a chocolate factory in the neighbourhood of what is now called Ghirardelli Square.

I certainly wasn't expecting the kind of starched atmosphere in the rural hinterland of California that I had sometimes met in London or Paris. Then I was still learning that America was the land of surprises, happy and otherwise. For instance, I had already met an altogether opposite image of social definition, a WASP one, when I was living earlier on the Hudson at Holy Cross. There I had encountered the monastery's next-door-neighbour in the person of the granddaughter of John Burroughs, the Catskill native, naturalist, author, and dear friend of Walt Whitman.

Her grandfather had been born in 1837, when the United States was still young. Her pride in him was immense as she showed me his Slabsides hideaway and talked of their life in Esopus, and I felt the spirit of Henry David Thoreau as well as Burroughs himself amid all that lush and sylvan beauty nestled in the heart of Upper New York State.

It was certainly a patrician family she sprung from — her being Episcopalian was as natural as the fall colours that dazzled my British eyes then for the first time — but she was only like her West Coast counterpart of Carmencita as far as being profoundly aware of her ancestry. Otherwise she was a dyed-in-the-wool Yankee with her own set of prejudices, such as her detestation of all Democrats and her belief that evil began with New York City and blossomed in Washington, D.C.

Back to Niven Busch! A very self-confident, even aggressive, man, he was also an ambivalent one. I felt that he would have been hard put to describe himself unequivocally as either as a novelist or a screenwriter. Although he contributed regularly to *The New Yorker* and wrote novels such as *California Street* and *Until the End of Time*, his primary reputation lay in his movie scripts, and of those, it was his westerns that won most acclaim. And like so many who achieve fame and even a concomitant fortune in one context, it is in a wholly other activity that true happiness lay.

I perceived the same disgruntlement in Busch as I had seen with Tom Matthews, Martha Gellhorn's caustic husband. And I think for comparable reasons. Perhaps it is the *déformation professionnelle* of a certain kind of novelist, but I sometimes feel I have been conditioned to listen to the shriek in a person's voice rather to the semantics of their words. It is a situation that over the decades I have found woefully

128

common — not least in successful writers for TV, media personalities such as Gilbert Harding, and journalists of all the media who excel in the highly contentious essay.

In previous, less complicated times when everything didn't have to be tested against the bar of psychological health the phenomenon might have been seen as one of true or false vocation. Then it is my suspicion that the affliction of being a square peg in a round hole is suffered silently by many in our society. And it is only the reasonably affluent, such as the likes of Niven Busch in the upper echelons of the movie industry, who can afford to be noisy and abrasive in their discontent.

# 22
# KENNETH REXROTH

For the first time in my life I felt a little odd in California: something of the outsider looking in. That is, until I started broadcasting regularly for radio station KPFA in Berkeley and meeting other writers who saw words as an art form and not merely as the utilitarian weapons of selling and entertaining.

I am sure it was my working on the Hearst flagship, the *San Francisco Examiner*, that put me on the outs with those who later in life would be regarded as my peers. I refer to the poets and playwrights, the Lawrence Ferlinghettis, Jack Spicers, and Robert Duncans of the Bay Area, the beat artists, the politically turbulent crowd associated with the Berkeley campus, the city jazz spots, and everything subsequently symbolized by the City Lights Bookstore and North Beach in general.

The world my work allotted me was symbolically situated at Third and Market, close enough to the downtown business sector. My colleagues were such as columnist Herb Caen, who came up with the popular slogan "Baghdad by the Bay" when Baghdad was not viewed as a connotation of evil but of romance. And conscientious music critic Al Reid and books editor Luther Nichols helped to preserve the image of the *Examiner* as culturally superior to the rest of the Hearst empire, as old Mrs. Hearst had always insisted it be.

Still in my time, in the early and mid-1950s, there were daily book reviews (to which I contributed) and total coverage of serious music, and I could do in-depth stories about the arts, whatever the manifestation, and however remote from the city's gates.

But yet ... but yet ... I was *still* soiled by the proximity of commerce, by dipping my pen in journalistic rather than creative ink. I, of course, knew that when not zipping about the state with photographer Tom King for my articles in the rotogravure section (a first, I believe) of the Sunday edition, or toiling in the *Examiner's* offices, I was busy in our apartment at the edge of the Marina completing my first novel. That was my effective armour against allegations of artistic corruption, for I had no awareness then of the fact that, although I had been accepted by a New York publisher, he was to subsequently blow his brains out in Greenwich Village, and that my book, finding no other sponsor, was destined to extinction.

But on those long Sunday afternoons at KPFA, I could meet those I regarded as peers of purpose if not of accomplishment. Among such stands out Kenneth Rexroth, poet and anarchist. During late 1958 and 1959 we regularly recorded our broadcasts with the Berkeley, California, listener subscription radio station KPFA.

Until I met Rexroth I thought *I* had the gift of the gab! Not that I ever believed I was so consummate in knowledge, so assured in wisdom, as he was. Then Kenneth was a poet and inhabited a world in which if the poet himself didn't believe he owned to a prophetic authority, then, sure as hell, no one else would! Indeed, most of their poetic peers seemed intent on murdering rival reputations.

To that poetic jungle – of which Kenneth Rexroth was a true inhabitant – one must also emphasize that he was a characteristic mid-century American poet, with the attendant traits that demanded. Not only were poets there, in California as elsewhere, marginalized and underestimated by their fellow citizens, they were often regarded with suspicion, if not downright hostility.

The air in those days still reeked of McCarthyism – especially towards those who didn't volubly extol capitalist enterprise, and even more for those who actually claimed to be anarchists. And given the conviction of the literary minority (certainly the poets and their hangers-on) that the American masses were utterly philistine and hostile to all artistic endeavour, the American poet had a quality of anger, of a self-conscious role that reminded me of the Old Testament prophets and had at that time no European counterpart, at least none of which I was aware. If I had not been already disqualified by my *Examiner* employment, the other banners that Rexroth held high could never be mine.

Soothsayers, gurus, shamans abounded at that time, and thus, long before the counterculture with its own contingent of sages and charlatans, KPFA was a haven to the genre.

Pacifism became freshly fragrant — even to those of us with blood-stained hands from the Second World War — and I became radical enough to step out on the sidewalk in front of the newspaper, as I identified with the American Newspaper Guild. Unfortunately, that act of defiance was distinctly short-term, as the strike (if such it was) was over in minutes and I was back at my desk in the features department as if nothing had happened. Repetition has not availed itself.

If my pacifism, distinctly rekindled by Rexroth, has remained a certain if intermittent hunger in my life, I have never responded in kind to his anarchism — or to that of my subsequent Canadian friend and mentor, George Woodcock. If I am truly of the right (rather than the left, that is), which sometimes, deep in the night, I seriously doubt, I am temperamentally capable of that final step towards libertarianism, as, at the end of the day, I abhor extremism more than anything else. The curse of that *via media* Anglican upbringing, no doubt.

Kenneth had no such brakes on his thinking or feeling. What's more, he had the volubility to clothe the most spontaneous and outrageous thoughts in words. That ability to think from the hip I have always admired though being unable to emulate. It certainly afforded me a lot of entertainment as we sat in the rather scruffy premises of the volunteer subscription radio station and I listened to Kenneth and others proclaim the Bay Area conscience in matters cosmic.

I so enjoyed that atmosphere at KPFA — okay, it was prone to go overboard now and then and react with Californian excess to every itch and bite on the body politic — that when I was sounded out as a possible successor as manager to the founder of the station, who had committed suicide about the time of my arrival in California, I was highly flattered. Those daydreams, however, were quickly extinguished when I learned that it was necessary to be an American citizen to occupy such a communications position. I'm not even sure whether the stipulation went as far as having to be a natural-born American. In any case, several years lay ahead before I could obtain citizenship, and the station, naturally, couldn't wait.

Then if all that had happened, I today would be an American rather than a Canadian and presumably still living in San Francisco rather than its equally glamorous sister to the north. I have always resisted the "if" game, which I think is really only a personal solace to the discontented.

# 23
# ROBERT PATCHELL

My editor at the *Examiner*, Bill Hall, was determined to expunge my British literary past in all haste. So within weeks, after a deluge of virulent memos had been tossed over the partition between our bordering offices, I had forsaken "kerb" for "curb," abandoned the plural for theatre cast and the government and embraced much older usages such as "gotten" and "dove." I also learned as a superogatory discipline — though this was harder — how to pronounce "vase" as "vaise." Shortening my *as* was jam compared to that!

The fact is I was not a little frightened by this bald-headed first-generation son of a Scot who boasted a glamorous mistress, Janet, on the very same floor of the *Examiner* building (she edited the newly born TV tab, which also came under his aegis), and whose quiet and economic grunts of speech were compensated by an acid content when it came to criticism or guidance of his neophyte employee. But like so many straight males in executive positions (not that I've known many!) his bark outweighed his bite. Perhaps I was made even more nervous by being gay; that and my immigrant ignorance and, above all, my English accent made me not only an exotic bird in his undisputed domain but a vulnerable one, too.

A dent in my apprehensions came when he very soon started to give me more and more interesting assignments, and if he was instant in criticism if I screwed up he was equally quick with praise for an article he considered well done. There was space for no middle-ground mediocrity in the magazine Bill Hall put out! I was soon off mere rewrites of standard publicity bumf and handling personal interviews or away with Tom King on my transstate travel pieces.

One in-town assignment that I found both instructive and amusing involved a prize-winning crucifix by a leading San Francisco artist. I was instructed to write about the giant crucifix, interview its creator, and get Tom to photograph it in a germane setting. The trouble was we couldn't find it. The artist himself was pretty sure that a local funeral parlour had it as a prop for its attendant mourners. But there were scores of undertakers along "funeral row" and we spent days searching for it from one house of repose to another. I learned of "viewing chambers," "comfort and solace rooms," "slumber chapels"— even of one place that boasted a deck on which the dead loved one could arrive by plane.

Yet the crucifix eluded us. Until one day a nervous mortician confessed he just might have what we were looking for. If we would step over to the broom closet?

It turned out that the crucifix, a twentieth-century update of an anguished Christ, all blood and gore, was far more than this San Francisco death disposal unit thought fitting for their customers' twentieth-century minds. So it had been relegated to the company of mops and buckets in a darkness where it could offend no tastes or lack of tastes. However, all was redeemed, and the massive crucifix was placed in a more congruous context and recorded for history in the pages of "Sunday Living" in the *San Francisco Examiner.*

My misgivings about Bill Hall's reaction to my living with Floyd in the Marina while he was doing his PhD at Stanford by commuting down to Palo Alto each day were also allayed when we received the alarming news that Floyd's mother, now living in Pacific Grove on the Monterey Peninsula, was about to go into hospital over an embolism that might conceivably be life-threatening.

I wanted just to make sure I remained in the city until the crisis was over but my boss said my place was with Floyd and that I should accompany him to Monterey. In fact, he insisted on it! As it happened, the operation was successfully accomplished, even before Floyd got there, and my spiritual mother-in-law went on to become an octogenarian. Bill Hall was as happy as I was.

But in one context I remained where I chronologically belonged: at the bottom of the heap. Each year all if us feature writers and reporters had the chance to become travel writers when the "junkets" were handed out. The whole world, it seemed, clamoured for gratis publicity from the Hearst organization, as well as other press media, of course, and there were opportunities to travel to and write articles on everywhere from Hong Kong and Australia to Vienna, London, and the Mountains of Mourne.

As the newcomer, however, I was offered none of these but instead a domestic Trailways bus tour to the Pacific Northwest: to Seattle, Victoria, and Vancouver, as the company was introducing uniformed women attendants serving meals en route — an obvious attempt to ape the airlines.

So it was that Floyd and I duly arrived in Vancouver, having "done" Seattle and Victoria (where I was able to see my old childhood friend of Cornish days, Natalie Guthrie) and found ourselves in the now extinct Grosvenor Hotel on a rainy Sunday afternoon. Having already read the Gideon Bible, I turned listlessly to the local telephone directory.

This was my first Sunday ever in a remote corner of an albeit dying empire and, indeed, the first time I had experienced a Puritanism that closed all movie houses on the Sabbath as well as public access to alcoholic beverages. My Methodist Cornwall seemed sin city in contrast!

As I flicked those pages of minuscule print and Floyd read, I don't doubt, something saner, I suddenly came across the initials CBC subsequently spelled out as Canadian Broadcasting Corporation and giving an address at the Hotel Vancouver, which I could see from our rain-splashed window.

The very next morning — I have suppressed how we survived the intervening hours — we arrived on the floor housing the CBC and I was ready with my questions of how, if in any way, did it resemble my old employer, the BBC. I now have a vague impression of countless young men shrieking in joy as they thumbed the pages of the past weekend's press and discovered a reference, positive or otherwise, to the CBC or one of its programs. But that may be a subsequent fantasy engendered by the quite erroneous allegation that the CBC was staffed to excess by high-strung faggots.

We were soon ushered into the presence of one serious, bespectacled youngish man (turned out later he was my age) who might have been a gay but certainly evinced nothing of a high-strung nature. His name was Robert Patchell and he was "Supervisor in Public Affairs" or some such magnificent CBC title. He was born in Carleton Place in the Ottawa Valley, a graduate of the University of Toronto (Victoria College), and was hoping to write the Great Canadian Novel — a term much in use in that era. I didn't find all that out in just that first talk between the three of us. But he subsequently asked us to lunch at a place I believe was called the Arctic Club and then persuaded us to stay an extra night, as he wanted to give a party for us at his apartment in the West End.

That gathering was mainly composed of gay CBC Radio staff, including at least three producers I came to know well over the years. I also met Annie-Laurie MacDonald, Bob's secretary, who was not only from the Maritimes but was the first Canadian I met who spoke Gaelic as her native tongue. That is how I came to appreciate the Canadian entity — bit by little bit, person by person.

Once in Vancouver I was enjoying a delicious tourtière by a hairdresser who claimed he was a Parisian. But I had become part of the family by then: I could easily ask him what part of Quebec he was from. Though that can lead to mini-traps. One of the best tourtière cooks I know, now a friend and a Vancouverite, honed his culinary skills on his mother's knee in Moncton, New Brunswick! In one of my earliest Canadian-based stories I was proud to include fiddlehead greens. It took me much longer to address gay carryings-on at Chalk River during the espionage-ridden era of the Manhattan Project.

Only a couple of weeks after our return to San Francisco, Bob called us to say that all CBC producers were on strike in protest to the Diefenbaker government's attacks on the corporation for left-wing bias in its parliamentary reportage. During his brief stay with us he must have duly noted both our growing library and record collection, for when, a year or so later, we were in New Brunswick, New Jersey, he called me and asked whether I would return to Vancouver to cover the music and theatre aspects of the newly created Vancouver International Festival, which was based on that of Edinburgh. I did and did again the following year. And have never left.

During those early years, when I was freelancing with the CBC, writing and publishing my first fiction, and Floyd had started as a lecturer in French literature at the University of British Columbia, we rapidly made our first Canadian friends to join those accumulated in the United States and in Britain and France before that. I am sure that is one reason we have been blessed with such a quantity as well as quality of boon friends over more than half a century.

# 24
# JANE RULE AND ETHEL WILSON

One of the few links with the Bay Area I had when moving to the Lower Mainland was the novelist Jane Rule. And that itself was something of a surprise. During our last dinner in San Francisco, Floyd and I celebrated with two guests. One of them was a fellow PhD candidate named Ellen Kay. I hadn't been in Vancouver many weeks when I was invited to the home of two women: said Jane and her partner, Helen Sonthoff. It was at their table that I heard Helen call Jane "Jinks" and sometimes "jinkus." I immediately recalled that the volume of her poems that Ellen Kay had given me in San Francisco was inscribed to "Jinks." I also remembered that the first poem described the beach along Point Grey. It didn't take me long to make the connection.

Ellen Kay left the Bay Area to return to New York — but not to be with her wealthy Jewish family but to become an Anglican nun in a strictly enclosed Franciscan order on Long Island. The community was later decimated by a Philippine cook who ran amok. Ellen next turned up in an Augustinian order of Episcopalians based in Poughkeepsie on the Hudson, the sister establishment, in fact, of the Order of the Holy Cross at West Park, further up the Hudson River from where I worked for its press, as described earlier in these pages. When I last saw her, in the home of the West Coast painter John Koerner, she was, I think, the prioress of the order's Seattle convent. She still maintained an epistolary connection with Jane Rule.

Over the years, Jane and I have been sometimes promoted as the male and female literary leaders of the West Coast gay community. Indeed, with the coming of the Gay Games to Vancouver in 1990 that was the official role assigned to us. I felt I was actually watching the city grow up when twenty thousand people marched into B.C. Place Stadium for that year's largest gay sporting and cultural event throughout the world. I was particularly happy to welcome the then federal minister of justice, Kim Campbell, who was eventually to become Canada's prime minister. At a more private level, we had a member of the gay Berlin soccer team staying in our home, and he told me that not only did buses slow down to pick up him and his fellow participants if wearing the official tag but that taxi drivers too provided free lifts to the various venues around the city to Hans and his gay competitors.

But Jane was far more personally involved with political activism — not just on behalf of lesbians and gays but for the women's movement generally. I always found her to be a person who moved easily in a wholly realized lifestyle — though in its quiet comfort, just this side of affluent, it was not one that everyone could emulate.

It is in her fiction that I am drawn most closely to her — paradoxically, because we are really so very different kinds of writers. She once remarked to me whereas I would bend over backwards to describe and place a tree in my fictional landscape, she would just step around it if it better suited her creative purpose. I think that sometimes there is also a hint of didacticism in her novels that is utterly absent from mine. Then Jane is far from being the only author who is also an instinctive teacher and whose pages can yield a blueprint to intelligent attitudes and action. I think I am more the incipient historian, anxious to describe the *what is* and the *what has been*, that is, to record a small but significant aspect of human life in literary fiction at a given period in time.

Whether we have achieved our respective goals is for others to say. All I want to recall is the fact of our friendship, of the laughter we two couples, one lesbian the other gay, shared, and the belief I have evolved that it is from such social and psychological margins as ours that an all-embracing vision of life is most clearly perceived.

Jane and her late and beloved Helen fulfilled yet another significant purpose for Floyd and myself. They ushered into our lives so many new friends. It is through them that we acquired entry into the creative constituency of our adopted city.

The first of these was not only a major Vancouver author but one of an international stature that I could attest from my very own childhood. A precocious adolescent, I was reading the British weekly the *New Statesman and Nation* when a schoolboy, and it was within its pages that I first read the stories of Ethel Wilson.

It was at the book party for Jane's first novel (and lesbian clarion call) *The Desert of the Heart* that I met the author of *Swamp Angel* and the collected short fictions *Mrs. Golightly and Other Stories* and became, if not a close friend, then a frequent companion in her later years, of the South African–born writer, now married to a pioneer doctor from the Okanagan Valley and retired to a sedate apartment house overlooking the metallic waters of English Bay.

In retrospect I believe that Vancouver was then small enough to facilitate broad jumps in the social and cultural category and that today such links as I describe here would be far more difficult if not impossible.

Ethel was a relative of what was considered an old Vancouver family, the Malkins, but she never made much of that in my presence. She was a down-to-earth old gal, with a slightly salty flavour to her speech, and further remarkable that for someone born in 1888 she couldn't care less about the sexual orientation of the likes of Jane and Helen or Floyd and myself. She was the daughter of a Methodist minister at that — then her English boarding school education in her teens and her subsequent teaching career and marriage in British Columbia represented vastly different influences on a young woman of the British Empire in those early years of the past century than I was to ever know at a comparable age.

An odd connection and flashback to my Days of Faith was inadvertently provided by Ethel's husband, Wallace, through a patient of his back in the early days when he was a pioneer physician in the Okanagan Valley. She was the mother of Father David Somerville, priest and rector of St. James's Church (and later archbishop of the Diocese of New Westminster), where I regularly worshipped when I first came to Vancouver. As I was talking one day to Mrs. Somerville in the Clergy

House — who was by then quite elderly, I might add — the name of Dr. Wilson came up.

I had recently been with him and Ethel in their apartment off Beach Avenue in the city's West End and a million miles from the Main and Hastings area, once the central core of the city and where the church was situated, but which, even then, was rapidly become ever more seedy and already attracting the drunk, the drugged, and the generally despairing.

On hearing the doctor's name the old lady informed me that it had been Dr. Wilson who had delivered her child up there in the Okanagan. He had asked her if she knew whether it was a boy or a girl. She claimed to have merely smiled at the physician and told him that of course she knew it was a boy. How could it be anything else when God had long ago told her that her son was destined to be a priest?

I felt a sense of biblical anecdote and image very close in that comfortable room adjacent to the Giles Scott–designed church, where I was closeted alone with a priest's mother, just a wall away from a raucous world where Skid Road was in the process of taking over.

All that remote reminiscence was jerked to a more unruly present when in November 2003 I happened to read an excerpt from a bio of Ethel by David Stouck. It gave me pause. The grammar is ambiguous but I'm not sure I was reading about the same Ethel Wilson I knew — and liked. To be sure, I have always found Wilson's fiction to be eminently satisfying and of a major order — even if often written in a minor key.

But the impression I had was never of a rather mannered "lady." I didn't find her vocal pitch remarkable and I was always impressed how this rather "square" woman, very much of her generation, reached out and admired the work of lesbian Jane. That alone singled out Ethel Wilson from many other women, as well as many men, of course, of not only Vancouver and not only that period in history.

To return to the Rule-Sonthoff phenomenon. What Jane and Helen managed to do, some forty or more years ago, was to provide Vancouver with the closest thing to a literary salon that it has ever known. Dozens of novelists, poets, and painters entered that rather unprepossessing little stucco bungalow in Point Grey. Here I met the likes of the super-prolific author George Woodcock, the poet Phyllis Webb, the shy, Ulster-born novelist Brian Moore, Canada's sardonic superstar Margaret Atwood, and Prairie-moulded Margaret Laurence, the novelist who became a good friend and of whom I will have more to say later.

The pattern continued when they moved to a more spacious house and eventually quit the mainland for a Pan-Abode residence, replete with swimming pool, on Galiano, one of the Gulf Islands scattered between Vancouver and Victoria. There they lived and flourished socially for the rest of the twentieth century and into the next.

There was booze offered at these gatherings but one seldom observed anyone worse for wear. Then both Jane and Helen had a little of the "blue stocking" in their makeup and high seriousness not only abounded but the two women hosts, amiable and considerate though they both always were as they weaved about the crowd making introductions and carrying beverages in the minuscule space, were disinclined to let their guests forget it.

If you had to push roles on the two of them, then you would have had to describe Helen as generally the more motherly of the two and Jane as the more "mannish." But I have seen those roles reverse in the twinkling of an eye — with Helen suddenly coming on as intellectually aroused thunder and Jane blinking owlishly through her glasses and pleading in her deep, contralto (basso?) voice for calm deportment amid their argumentative guests and the need for social cohesion and peace.

Jane might wear pants but they did not dress in anything like a self-conscious, Sapphic manner. Nor was there in those days a lot of conversation along the lines of sexual liberation. Rather was the thrust of talk towards the threat of philistinism, political and otherwise, and the need of the creative artist to affirm values and refuse submission to the wooing of governments, local or national, and the affirmation of structures that would serve the arts generally.

I would stress "generally," for in fact, apart from the writers likely to be present (who relied less on physical amenities and more on subsidies and grants), Jane and Helen also ensured that many of their guests were from the *visual* arts. In fact this was a distinctive element to these soirees. Not composers or musicians — I think our hosts were generally tone deaf and I certainly don't recall a single lengthy conversation confined to serious music. But painters and sculptors were definitely very central to the lives of these two women and the walls of their house(s) fully reflected the fact, with the canvases of local artists such as Gordon Smith, John Koerner, Jack Shadbolt, and Tak Tanabe competing for space. All these men and their wives we first met under the Jane/Helen roof and in every case the couples became our good friends — remaining so until death or departure to other places took them out of our Vancouver lives.

Jane Rule's impact was informing not only of my life but of my family's too. Once, when back in Cornwall visiting my mother when she was ninety or thereabouts, I happened to enter her bedroom to retrieve something she'd requested. On her dressing table, amid silver framed photos of my father mounted on his camel when he was in the Imperial Camel Corps in Palestine, one of her younger brother, Claude, killed in the Great War, and others of me and my two brothers, was also a signed one of Jane.

# 25

# JACK AND DORIS SHADBOLT
# AND A VANCOUVER CIRCLE

y initial encounter with the Shadbolts, tweedy husband and smartly dressed spouse, painter and curator, wasn't exactly the warmest. I'm a little hazy about the chronological specifics but I'm pretty sure it was when both of them and Floyd and I were once more dinner guests of Jane Rule and her partner, Helen Sonthoff. That would have been in the 1960s when the two latter literary women still lived in Point Grey, taught at UBC, and hadn't migrated to Galliano Island. Jack looked rather like a tall if substantial English squire — with that slightly bucolic look one associates with the Shires rather than his native Shoeburyness. Not that the balding man with piercing eyes and a rounded face, which was never devoid of a necktie below it, sounded other than the western Canadian he was, being only four when he arrived here.

Neither Shadbolt was hostile, but without wishing to sound paranoid I thought them distinctly reserved — and I mean more than just the general Canadian disposition that had, along with the bright lights in bars, been a mild cultural shock for someone coming up from volatile and extrovert California.

At that 1950s and early 1960s period in Vancouver's cultural, social, and political evolution, if you were gay, had a British accent, and were also a new boy on the block, it wasn't altogether surprising to encounter among one's peers or possible competitors a raised eyebrow or a subtle lowering of the corners of the mouth. I was once screamed at by a fellow scribe, an ex-sportswriter and a devotee of strictly amateur theatre who wanted to share my role as the *Vancouver Sun*'s official drama critic, as I was "a goddamned queer who'd parachuted into paradise and was determined to corrupt and ridicule everything in sight."

Again, when through a bureaucratic boo-boo I was assigned from my New York base, together with a critic from Winnipeg, to cover the musical events of the Vancouver Festival, instead of coming to an arrangement with me to divvy up the items to be covered, or even agreeing that I would confine myself to the theatre events (which I had also been offered and which I was perfectly prepared to do), my fellow reviewer refused to meet me, or even speak to me, throughout the duration of the festival.

At the time I told myself that he simply had problems of a personal nature, but now I know I was guilty of total ignorance of the colonial or ex-colonial attitude that was then common in Canada. I saw myself just as David Watmough, who had been invited up from the United States to do what I had been doing in San Francisco for my newspaper, radio, and, as far as books were concerned, also for the *New York Times*. That is, "feeding my habit" as a yet unpublicized and thus unpaid novelist and short story writer.

But Ken Winters didn't see it as that at all. He heard my British accent and had already been informed that I had been a BBC arts producer and had reviewed for such London journals as the *Spectator* and *Time & Tide*. And when I got the same financially attractive as well as prestigious assignment as he, a Manitoba-born, established Winnipeg critic, how it must have stung to be if not exactly ousted but made as a Canadian to share with an outsider, a foreigner, who had hardly spent five minutes in his country!

It was an attitude I was to meet many times and to sense it operating when I didn't specifically confront it, both as a freelancer and eventually as an author in Vancouver and Toronto. But I learned to accept it as part of the cost of the immigrant experience. Gradually becoming a Canadian, learning to cherish the specifics of Canada, made it all well worth it. Indeed, with my later novels when I was a little older, I was able to make use of the experience in my fiction. I count it among my blessings to be an immigrant Canadian and especially at a time when these matters were far from being taken for granted.

Even after many years of possessing a Canadian passport and being proud of the fact, I was told by a fellow writer, a woman in her thirties, that I wasn't a *real* Canadian like herself, who was born in British Columbia. In vain did I insist that her citizenship was an accident of where she fell from a womb whereas mine was a matter of election. She remained adamant in her conviction that I could never be as Canadian as she. Bitchily I resorted to listing famous Canadians of foreign birth such as our honoured humorist Stephen Leacock, Ethel Wilson, Sir John A. Macdonald, and musician Healey Willan. But I hadn't gotten too far with my illustrious roster before she resorted to an international device to end all argument and burst into tears. She later told our genial Aussie host that she had been low in argumentative stamina because she was having her period.

Even so, such xenophobia, though always greater here than in the United States, remained the exception rather than the rule and certainly the Shadbolts were in no way a part of it. (Then, come to think of it, Jack Shadbolt was born in England, Gordon Smith was a fellow Brit, and the third in that trio of artists united roughly by age and eminence, John Koerner, was a native Czech.) But I think, nevertheless, I was perceived by Jack and Doris as a brash newcomer, too full of opinions, and, worse sin yet, believing that words were inherently superior to paint. For Jack, at least, it was a paradoxical position, for he had more than a little belief in himself as a poet earlier in life and, as all who knew him would attest, he was never at a loss for words.

If such were the kinds of thoughts going through the heads of the painter and his wife, they were definitely not expressed that night. As usual when in his company, Doris, I think the intellectually superior, was muted. Ditto at that period for many wives of local prominent men! The only exception that I met in my early days in Canada was the distinguished refugee from Ontario, Lawren Harris, and his second wife, Beth, who was not only an energetic theosophist seeking conversions but every inch his equal in intelligence and articulation. Though even she, come to think of it, didn't compete with her husband in the social situations I experienced in their house overlooking English Bay and the then dark and daunting North Shore Mountains, which were still devoid of suburban housing and not yet festooned at night with domestic electricity.

Jack Shadbolt was prone to centre his vocal boom upon the perpetual friction between the regional art scene and that of the East, and even more fiercely on the patronizing attitudes exhibited by the Toronto- and Ottawa-based media towards all creative activity on the West Coast, his own not excepted. Then he was already an assured and powerful painter and such condescension must surely have been galling.

Compared with him, Gordon Smith was quiet, almost reclusive — then his art, too, reflected a lyricism that transferred easily from formal to abstract and behind which lurked the ghost of the English watercolourists. I soon picked up on the links discernible between the art and the artist. I can hear his dry yet gentle tones as I glance up at his pictures surrounding me in my study as I work.

It was particularly through Gordon and his wife that I first developed an avid thirst for the immediate history of the place where Floyd and I had come to live. Gordon would tell stories of long-ago romantic activities at teenage dances in a hotel on Bowen Island that subsequently burned down. Marion, on persuasion, would evoke her childhood in British Columbia's first white settlement of Sapperton and adjacent New West-minster, where she had known as fellow adolescents both the figurative painter Joe Plaskett, whose dad had been rector of the Anglican parish, and Sheila Watson, the author of the novel *The Double Hook*.

I thrilled to have those pre-war days and the early postwar days en-fleshed by these two rather quiet people living in their disconcertingly transparent Arthur Erickson home, where they were intimately observed only by the likes of squirrels, raccoons, and ravens, and otherwise snugly screened amid the bushes and tall trees on the fringes of lush Lighthouse Park in a then relatively uninhabited West Vancouver.

We visited often and those encounters were very precious. It is not mere fancy to see echoes of so much of Gordon's work in the coastal colours and turbulent vegetation that surround his extensively glass-windowed home. Our love of the teeming animal and bird life about them was yet a further bond.

Jack Shadbolt nursed a dramatic element in his personality that isn't only facilely seen in his canvases as a war artist during the Second World War but is inherent in his intriguing owls and animals as well as in the series that issued from a Canada Council grant to the Aegean — *The Space Between the Pillars*, in which hover the ghostly white pillars of ancient Greek temples.

John Koerner's paintings, large and small, are all hushed and lyrical poems in comparison. Then there is a definite metaphysical link here between the quiet-voiced man and the elegiac work. There is another factor too that determines a certain reticence, a distillation in Koerner's canvases compared with those of the other two.

For many years Koerner's reputation ranked less than theirs. Partly, I'm convinced, not because the work, per se, is less worthy but because he had to fight a prejudice from the local cognoscenti of critics and patrons. He was the son of a comparatively rich immigrant family of lumber barons who created and owned B.C. Forest Products. A poor little rich boy, you might say, who therefore didn't deserve the plaudits owing to those of less wealthy backgrounds. I always thought it a little irony that, perhaps in subconscious reaction to all that, John Koerner offered his works at significantly higher prices than those of his confreres. I admired that and sometimes wish we authors had some say in the price of our books. I think there would be some surprises.

I saw quite a bit of Shadbolt at the Bau-Xi Gallery, where all three men then exhibited and whose owner, Paul Wong, had fast become a friend of mine and who actually published my one and only volume of plays. At the same time I was also seeing Jack at the then Vancouver Art Gallery, whose bulky and jocular director, Fred Amiss, had even more fluent words at his disposal than Jack did!

As a result of getting to know Fred when I officially became visual arts critic for the *Vancouver Sun*, he asked me to give the graduation address at the then newish Vancouver Playhouse for his art school students. The first to respond to that solo performance (at which I may say I was distinctly nervous) was blunt Jack Shadbolt. He came striding down the crowded auditorium, his arm outstretched. It was right then that I knew I now had overcome a prejudice and made a friend.

With Doris, who was infinitely more shy than her husband, my sense of moving from acquaintance to friend took place at the Vancouver Art Gallery—in her office. I'd been appointed the *Sun*'s art critic, and although I visited her for an ostensible interview it was essentially to seek her advice and ensure I could go to her whenever the local current art scene seemed beyond my ken. She met my overture with instant warmth and help, and from then on I knew I could forget any nonsense about "artists' wives" and enjoy her for her own true worth and impressive knowledge. That may sound odd to younger ears but I cannot stress too much what efforts were still then necessary for women to achieve equal voice — with the corollary that men, even gay ones like me, also had to learn to overcome the self-appointed boundaries that women like Doris had learned to live with in terms of their marriages, and thus to respect a mind for its steel rather than its gender. So important was that lesson for me that it in large part inspired the nonagenarian in my novel *The Moor Is Dark Beneath the Moon* and much more of my fiction since 2002, when that book was published.

# 26
# MARGARET LAURENCE

Margaret Laurence shared far more with me than a common birth date. We both loved to carouse, we both thrilled to the sound and shape of the English language, and we both admired each other. And she as long-time émigré in Britain and Africa and I as maple leaf newcomer were, when we met in the 1960s, both excited about the fresh stirring in Canadian letters and in the new shaping of literary life across our vast and (from my then still European eyes) under-populated country.

In fact it was Margaret who first made me truly aware of my status as an accepted Canadian author in a specially warm and comforting way. Then without being gushy or superficial, she had a way of praising and encouraging that uniquely benefited the tentative, even timorous, writer — let alone one who had only just nailed his colours to the national mast. Not that she was always in agreement with me, any more than she was with anyone else. I found it fascinating in coincidence to discover in the volume that houses some of her letters to me (*A Very Large Soul: Selected Letters from Margaret Laurence to Canadian Writers*, edited by J.A. Wainwright) that she also corresponded at length with my old California friend Will Ready after he'd become librarian at McMaster University. She, a dyed-in-the wool Prairie product with the United Church in her veins, was writing Roman Catholic Will Ready about the Mass and the prayers associated with the Blessed Virgin Mary!

Her Prairie influences extended in measure to her populism. She was too canny to transfer all her background into trite political stances — even her vigorous and staunch feminism was regulated by her intellect and sense of proportion — all of which was meat and drink to me. But there were areas where she thought I wasn't radical enough and she never hesitated to point it out. Margaret was no fool, and perhaps she was that rare kind of angel who had no fear of rushing in anywhere or, for that matter, at any time.

While I was staying with her once in her little cabin on the Otonabee River, near Peterborough, Ontario, she elected to discuss the expected behaviour she sought of me that evening when we were to be entertained by neighbours who were neither writers nor "intelligentsia" in any sense. These were salt-of-the-earth folk, she made perfectly clear, who meant as much to her as would have William Shakespeare and Johann Wolfgang von Goethe, had those guys happened to have been living next door. So would I please mind my P's and Q's and not come on all "literary."

The result was a rare experience of social farce that has provided me and my friends with amusement from that day to this. Before we found ourselves wandering over a dew-saturated lawn where someone in our trio (which apart from Margaret and I included playwright Michael Mercer) lost a now sodden shoe and arriving at one of the nine nearby cabins ("shacks," I think Margaret called them) where the party was to be held, I was given a further long lecture about how an author — "one of the tribe," as she was wont to say — should behave before an honest artisan who was a proud printer and equal in his fashion to an Albert Einstein, and certainly to a David Watmough!

This was not offered in a hostile fashion. Put simply, Margaret was a fundamental egalitarian and, I suspect, had been pained in the past by some cerebral friend patronizing one of her unlettered pals whom she revered for other reasons than scribbling.

We were no sooner in the house when we were taken by Tom and Irene, our hosts, into the living room. On the mantelpiece above the unlit fireplace was a large fish tank with a strangely immobile fish taking up most of its space. Curious, I wandered forward to investigate. At which point, I think a further light was switched on, because now the fish glowed. "Hello," it said. "I am a muskellunge and I weigh fifteen pounds. I was caught by Tommy in the Otonabee River on May 12, 1971 ..." My smothered laughter blots out the remaining statistics. It wasn't until much later in the proceedings that I dared to have Michael Mercer explain to a mind so radically untutored in technology that there was a tiny tape player in the pike's mouth that provided all the angler's pride and data at the flick of a switch.

But such technological prowess was not the only delight of that evening when, at Margaret's firm bidding, I was still was on my best behaviour. In a further room there was arranged a buffet table crammed with fishy foodstuffs harvested from the adjacent canals and rivers, and amply backed up with splendid salads and magnificent cream-garlanded desserts. It was the latter that stand out in my recollection. Before we were summoned to dig in, there was dancing encouraged in the minuscule space in front of the food-crammed tables. Several middle-aged couples essayed the foxtrot or the quickstep. Margaret and I remained applauding observers. It was my young friend, later to be the author of the renowned play so prophetically entitled *Goodnight Disgrace*, who, to prevent himself stumbling, and before gallantly dancing with his already radically weaving hostess, reached out a hand to steady himself. Unfortunately it found itself sinking into a large bowl of creamed trifle or the like. Horrified, Michael rapidly replaced it, fingers outstretched as we could clearly see, across the bare back of the printer's wife. That she neither flinched from the cold whipped cream nor felt its substance trickle down within her skirt was a tribute, I am now certain, to the warming and numbing influences of the rye she had drunk, was drinking, and would continue to drink for the rest of the festive evening.

There was a postscript that allows me to allude for the final time to alcohol in the context of my friend and protagonist, my dearest Margaret. Back at her own shack, she suggested a nightcap. And after Michael had served all three of us Scotches, hers neat, ours with soda, she elaborated at length and in knowing detail of the worthiness of the Scottish beverage and, indeed, of its pre-eminence over all other beverages to be found across our great land.

Perhaps ebullient over my good behaviour next door, or just relaxed and convivial as she invariably was with friends, she went further, allowing that as far as she was concerned, all other drinks tasted like horse piss and she unvaryingly rejected the whole bloody lot. Unfortunately, it was at that very moment that the fates decreed we had run out of her delectable potion. There was no Scotch left. Only a bottle of rye, a gift from her dear friend and father of her godson, Daniel, her bearded Don Bailey, who at that time was living in the shack adjacent to hers. Without a second's hesitation, and without the trace of a flinch, on being told the dreadful news, Margaret decreed that the rye be opened. I could see the resolution in those dark eyes. Tragedy was to be averted at all costs that precious summer evening where one could hear the water lapping and yet be safe from the marauding mosquitoes hovering outside.

It was steadily consumed, even with a smacking of hostess lips — though that may have been out of gratitude to Don rather than innate appreciation of the liquor — and with the conversation moving to the still young Writers' Union of Canada (TWUC) and Margaret's hopes and misgivings on that score.

It has become a commonplace observation that writers' friendships thrive best on mutual admiration. In my case that is far from true. There are authors whose work I esteem yet over whom I am personally ambivalent. Among those I would include the late Dorothy Livesay, whose poetry I often admire while her opinions, not least her facile political ones, I generally thought idiotic. I should add in fairness that the contempt in that case was mutual; in her later years, I once walked into a restaurant in Victoria, and on seeing me, she wrapped her cloak about her and marched out! We also had a public shouting match at a meeting in downtown Vancouver when she stung my Cornish pride by dismissing me contemptuously as a carpetbagging Welshman!

Not that Margaret and I always agreed on every possible topic. True, she had a marvellous and innate sense of coast-to-coast Canada that I found refreshing. Of course, she had lived on the coast as well as in Ontario — apart from being Prairie-born and spending substantial time in England and Africa. Then Margaret Atwood, superstar of the eastern Canadian literary circus, and in accent and attitude so redolent of Upper Canada, had also spent time in Vancouver. There is where I first met her — again in the famous Jane Rule context — but from social encounters there to the literary venues provided by the Writers' Union of Canada, I have never felt she has any real sense of western Canada or of the need for compromise and forbearance when it comes to transcending the unease and friction of our unruly federation.

The spontaneous sense of kinship I experienced with the other Margaret finds its genesis in several shards of shared experience as well as a genuine attraction to each other's fiction, which is contingent upon taste and an overall literary experience. But beyond the bookish link were always such matters as a common awareness of how informing loneliness can be. Margaret Laurence is often referred to in the context of her now famous description of us Canadian writers as a tribe. But her sense of the tribe is also concomitant, I'd suggest, with an awareness of life *outside* the tribe: that of the ardent but still unpublished writer, the uprooted anywhere, the orphan and the refugee.

These were states that Margaret Laurence had either experienced or had sensed their proximity — as I had done, too. And they, apart from the mutual admiration over the fruits of our creativity, were steel bonds joining us in a close and informing friendship.

Margaret was a novelist I rank with my childhood hero, D.H. Lawrence, a woman who knew the paramount importance of roots, a cognizance reflected wonderfully in her novel *The Stone Angel* and culminating in *The Diviners*.

She was also a tremendously *loyal* friend, and that, you may well believe, strengthened even more our mutual Celtic alliance. And may I say, quite unabashedly and in the same vein of high seriousness of which she was pugilistically capable, my comrade-in-letters was also — fun.

# 27
# PIERRE ELLIOTT TRUDEAU

How I ever got involved specifically with the licensing of FM radio stations with the federal government's recently created Canadian Radio-television and Telecommunications Commission I have now forgotten, if I ever knew! What I do recall is the ebullient bureaucrat in Ottawa asking me whether I objected to dining with the prime minister. When I offered her a puzzled "no" she went on to add that it would be at an inexpensive little Jewish family restaurant with jokey old Abe Rabinovitch providing personal service, a tucked-away place that the prime minister frequented and to where she liked to take out-of-town visitors such as myself.

Apart from a slight sense of unease over the slightly patronizing description — ever heard anyone refer to a rather pricey little Jewish restaurant favoured by the elite but with lousy service? — I was really impervious to the other clientele. She was to explain the federal system of licensing distribution, especially how it made an impact on British Columbia. And I was there in the capital as a British Columbia writer representative of the Association of Canadian Radio and Television Artists, and the union was keen to see what employment possibilities it would have for our B.C. membership. I had made this kind of trip across the country enough times already to divide Canada up in terms of *realpolitik* into "Upper," "Lower," "Western," and finally British Columbia as "Outer"! Also, when there in Ottawa I always had the anecdote burning in my ears of the time my friend Michael Mercer was told by a Toronto CBC producer that if he wanted to be taken seriously as a major writer he better go live in the Big

T. The small irony of that was that Michael was a refugee from "Cincinnati North," as we were wont to call the Lake Ontario city, and was to end up doing major commissions such as heading the writers' team for the American TV adaptation of *Lonesome Dove* and other major firsts for Canadian playwrights and authors electing to live in British Columbia.

But my Ottawa hostess was a pleasant woman, the food good, and my West Coast paranoia temporarily laid to rest. We had just sat down when the proprietor, in a stage whisper, announced to our table that the prime minister and his party were just arriving. And so, on the opposite side of the very small room eventually sat Pierre Trudeau, his wife, three small boys, and a couple I immediately saw were the grandparents, the Sinclairs from Vancouver.

I was struck, as I had been years before on seeing Prime Minister Atlee as I walked to King's in London, at how the political heads of the two countries went their ways without benefit of a whole posse of armed guards or secret service as protection. There was no one in the dining area of the restaurant with the prime minister and his family. I also remembered Eric Abbott, when dean of Westminster Abbey, telling me that when President Nixon attended a service in the abbey, U.S. secret servicemen not only filled the pews but, to his decanal chagrin, skulked about the ancient rafters and flit to and fro on the leads of the medieval roof in their determination to protect their president from all ill in that venerable House of God.

Thanks to a diligent mother I am neither a starer nor a pointer — both actions being frowned upon by her Victorian mentors — but I nevertheless discreetly observed from the outside position of our table bench that it was Pierre, not Margaret, who carefully cut the little boys' food into small pieces — while the retired senator and his spouse merely scowled at the world and stolidly ate from their plates. The prime minister's wife smiled prettily across at us, the only other diners, and exuded her pleasure with the moment.

Not that the moment lasted very long. Soon Justin and Sacha — Michel was still too much a baby — came running across to us. They spoke in unison and in English: "That's our daddy over there. He's the prime minister." What more they might have blurted I shall never know, for at that moment M. Trudeau arrived — to apologize and reclaim his charges.

On their return to their seats things continued as if there had been no youthful bolting from their table. Pierre returned to the task of cutting up their food, Margaret continued to primp and smile, while the older Sinclairs just kept on scowling. It is a charmingly human icon of our First Family that I will treasure through the years. It also meant that I knew no surprise when the couple duly divorced – even less to learn that our prime minister retained the custody of the three boys.

Maybe there is something about national capitals that aren't much else that gets into people, a kind of bitchy humour that somehow obviates the sheer boredom of a place like Ottawa and, I'm told, Canberra. In any case, it was again Ottawa and at one of our Writers' Union of Canada annual general meetings that I overheard the following comment, which, given it was among writers of greater and lesser eminence, might have been stirred as much by envy as by malice. Canada's leading literary lady was present, dressed, I recall, in some kind of Scottish plaid affair. With her was her then infant daughter, somewhat similarly attired.

"Is that Peggy Attwood?" a demure voice behind my shoulder inquired.

"I think so," came a contralto collaboration.

There was a slight pause for deliberation before voice number one mused, "My goodness, she has certainly shrunk since our last annual general meeting." And a hand followed the voice as it pointed not at Peggy but at the little girl.

That of course was not intended as a prophetic announcement but, in hindsight, I am tempted to think it forestalled a change in the union over the years – perhaps a dilution of that sense of literary tribalism that Margaret Laurence had unerringly seized upon in the early days of our genesis. Partly, of course, an age factor takes its toll on travellers to annual general meetings scattered across the second largest country in the world. But I also think that there is often a constituent of bruised egos when writers flushed or withered by a surfeit or drought of critical recognition are forced into coming together. And to compound matters, the plethora of medals, awards, and prizes that has come about for the writing community internationally and turned it into a kind of ludicrous Olympic Games has done nothing to serve fraternal unity or quell the unceasing persistence of the literary green eye.

# 28
# ROBIN SKELTON

Robin Skelton, I came to believe, was more of a mixture than most of us. I met him in the early 1970s through the Writers' Union, and although I knew him in his home base of Victoria and spent time in his house, our most informing hours were those we shared when in the East at TWUC meetings or conferences. In my contribution to his Festschrift *Skelton at 60*, edited by Barbara Turner (1986), I referred to my friend as "this odd amalgam." I won't push this factor too far as it might arrive at a quality of inconsistency. And I am too aware of what Robin Skelton and I had in common to be overly happy with that.

Superficially what we shared is as follows. Just under a year older than me, this British transplant arrived in Canada at roughly the same period. We were both intent on re-rooting as West Coast British Columbians, and, as in the case of Margaret Laurence, there was the glue of mutual appreciation of each other's work. We also shared in the vituperation of Dorothy Livesay, as he, too, was attacked by her as a pseudo-Canadian who should defer to the tastes and (more importantly) to the ego of her Manitoban self.

Even though Robin was a Yorkshireman and spent the British part of his career in Manchester, he early on found a fascination with such Celtic factors as Ireland to match my Cornish self-consciousness. It is not without significance for me, at least, that the photo taken by the poet Susan Musgrave that adorns the front cover of *Skelton at 60* is of Robin prostrate at Lanyon Quoit, a famous Celtic landmark in Cornwall.

Of course, he was straight and I was homosexual. He was the father of three and I was childless. And in those constituents, or rather from them, I learned some lesser known aspects of the bearded, twinkle-eyed poet who spent more time on composing and perfecting his assured public persona than anyone else I have known. For instance, although he never stated it directly, I am convinced that his son, Nick, who had gone to live in London, was gay, and that he had contracted HIV-AIDS. It was not, I believe, because Robin was in denial about his son's sexual identity but rightly felt that it was the boy's own business. And who can judge someone for being reticent over someone they loved very much being threatened, far from home, with a life-threatening illness? Not me. Oh, yes, Robin, loquacious and laughter-erupting Robin, could be quite discreetly circumspect if he felt the circumstances warranted it.

Yet there was another subject over which he was distinctly reticent that I found harder to explain — not least because on our frequent travels we talked of everything under the sun and not excluding matters of gossip and highly privileged information. We were peers on that score! But over South African–born John Peter, co-founder with Robin of *The Malahat Review*, colleague, and at least a one-time friend, a drawbridge was eventually thrown up. Peter, who has been badly served by the country of his adoption (there is no mention of him in any major or, for that matter, minor reference book I have come across), won the Doubleday Canadian Novel Prize for his 1964 *Along That Coast* and in 1967 published *Take Hands at Winter*, which I also enjoyed.

I do not wish to make an excessive mystery over it, but I met Robin and John Peter together on a TWUC trip back east, and although the latter was always sombre and inclined to be morose that in no way prevented the three of us becoming friends and enjoying each other's company on these annual trips, which were abruptly cut off by John's premature death a few years later.

Of that, too, Robin had little to say, and what he did was not particularly compassionate. Then these two talented writers had had a falling out and although I am inclined to give Robin the benefit of the doubt, as he explains their rift in his *The Memoirs of a Literary Blockhead*, I am fully aware that both were stubborn and that Robin was genuinely distressed on learning that John Peter was dying in hospital. But I had long ago taken unto myself the adage of St. Paul in Ephesians 26: "Let not the sun go down upon your wrath." For more than fifty years my lover and I have asked each other for forgiveness each night in bed before turning over to sleep.

Robin Skelton was yet another of those men who had considerable success in masking his shyness. Then he was so multi-faceted, what with his love of warlock lore, his affection for cemeteries, his very real concern for and participation with the visual arts, his prose pieces, his editorial work, and, of course, his poetry, that, to put it mildly, he was a difficult gent to pin down.

He was also a genuinely generous man, prepared to put himself out to help another, even if he was never unaware of some possible advantage that the good deed might procure for him. Then I call that sensible, as I have never understood enlightened self-interest to be a pejorative stance whether applied to individuals or nations.

One example of Robin's generosity led unforeseeably to a rupture with a married couple and a sudden ugly awareness that the suppression and distortion of vital truths can flourish even in rather isolated and generally agreeable places. Robin had agreed to host the Vancouver Island book launch for my novel *The Time of the Kingfishers* (so it must have been four years before his death in 1997) at a bookstore. The day after the launch, which was a Saturday, Floyd and I were invited to lunch with an ex-Vancouver couple. We were through the entrée and about to embark on the dessert when our rather whiny-voiced hostess asked me whether I had read a recent book by Gitta Sereny. Of course I had — and proceeded to tell her that Gitta was an old friend. The woman then informed me that the book (which was about Albert Speer, whom Gitta had known well and had interviewed) was full of falsehoods. And that there was no mention of all the little German boys that had been deliberately murdered by the Allies in the aftermath of the Second World War. It wasn't long before she was denying the Holocaust had ever happened and elaborating the rest of the drivel favoured by anti-Semites and their ilk.

We said little more save to insist she was talking nonsense and simply got up from the unfinished meal and quickly left the house. I have never darkened their door again but have certainly made it my mission to inform every ear I can find that a malevolent crypto-Nazi lurks in innocent Victoria! There is enough in the history of the twentieth century relating to the treatment of the Jews by Gentiles to shame every one of us for at least another century to come. And a whitewashing of the facts merely preserves the stench without a vital nurturing of the memory of what a century earlier Robert Burns so prophetically called "man's inhumanity to man."

# 29
# THE BENCH PARTY

I t began in the simplest manner possible. Floyd and I were celebrating our fortieth anniversary and, unknown to us, a group of friends decided to commemorate the event by having a bench erected in our memory in Jericho Park in the city of Vancouver, quite close, in fact, to where we have lived for more than thirty years. When I first saw it — still unaware of its existence until that moment — I thought momentarily that we had died and were looking down at our memorial bench from wherever! But the actual words inscribed on the plaque implied we were still alive.

With the arrival of that bench in Jericho, a new tradition entered our lives. Thanks to two further friends in Vancouver, Barbara Shumiacher, a woman of singular dramatic ingenuity, and her husband, Judah, a man of singular patience, an annual party is held al fresco at the site of the bench. There is simple fare — it is an afternoon event — and it is high-lighted by readings from those of us present: me reading from whatever novel or story I am currently writing; the others whatever has struck them as interesting from what they have recently read.

As it takes place in late summer it has often seen guests from afar, such as my cousin Margaret from the Cornish moors, who now lives in Stony Brook, Long Island, with her husband and son. Another guest grac-ing our little proceedings has been octogenarian Mary Filer, that rarity, a Vancouver native, and one who has become a distinguished and much sought after artist in glass. Her work graces the foyer of the Simon Fraser University downtown premises and Harbourfront, as well as homes, churches, cathedrals, and civic institutions around the globe. I know of no one who is a better example of how to carry the weight of accumulated time with such dignity and grace. She is truly a beacon for the darkness of the yet unknown geriatric years.

I have seen the oddest expressions on people's faces as they have passed our cluster crowding the bench and assorted collapsible chairs on our yearly observance. And if they happen to come down the path when the readings are going on (some of them quite dramatic and inviting commensurate actions from the reader) the looks of the passersby have turned from bewilderment to outright alarm! I guess we could be taken as a huddle of religious enthusiasts at worship or an even more arcane gathering. At the very first of these celebrations I recall that Barbara and Judah read from Cervantes's *Exemplary Novels*, where two dogs, Plato and his friend, discuss the oddities of their human masters when the latter have retired for the night. And that insightful and humorous text was so magnificently rendered by the seated Shumiachers that I actually saw one passerby break from a leisurely stroll into a panicky run as he fled past our scene.

But the bench also plays another role for me — one to which I'm sure the kind sponsors never gave a thought. So many of the benches in Vancouver, particularly but not exclusively in Stanley Park, are memorials to those who died of AIDS during the plague years. I didn't know all of them, of course, but a sad number were friends or acquaintances. And like so many gay survivors, even without the aid of a donated park bench to provide an extra nudge, there is still the almost daily thought once expressed by the sixteenth-century divine, John Bradford, on seeing some criminals taken to their execution: "But for the grace of God, there goes John Bradford." The major difference being that while I am alive to write these words in my eighties, poor John was burned at the stake in Smithfield in 1555 as a heretic when he was forty-five.

The other sense of personal good fortune associated with our bench in Jericho is the fact that both those responsible for its erection and those who join us in our yearly celebration are by far and large heterosexual friends. I have indeed come a long way from imprisonment in His Majesty's Winchester Prison as a gay offender back in 1944 when I was barely seventeen.

Among the friends dead from AIDS whom I covertly commemorate whenever I pass by our bench is one who only once visited us in Vancouver, was born in Philadelphia, and died in Los Angeles. Who was a dancer/choreographer and who was black. I first met Paul Reid Roman on a train from Toronto to Stratford, Ontario, where his lover, an actor, was performing. We subsequently met again in Ottawa when I was there attending TWUC meetings and several times in Los Angeles where he lived.

Paul choreographed the big auto company shows that started in Detroit and travelled elsewhere in conjunction with the promotion of new car models. That was a tough, competitive world — then Paul was a tough, competitive person. At a deeper level I don't think it excessive to describe him as an essentially *angry* person.

Not that his seething non-acceptance of the black man's lot — let alone the *gay* black man's lot — in any way mitigated other constituents that jostled for room in his complex, if mercurial, character. He was as generous in mind as he was in the disposition of this world's goods. Even while moving from growling to exploding in his little West Hollywood home as he entertained a handful of friends at dinner, he would be thanked for a financial gift by this one, for arranging a job interview by that one. And their social range varied from a poor black girl who had come to him by streetcar from Long Beach to some fairly affluent Hollywood personality involved with dance or ballet. I was by no means the only white person at these gatherings but the majority was African-American like himself, though not, for the most part, from a middle-class Philadelphian home as he was.

Paul was the only black person with whom I was able to develop a real relationship over the years — though I will confess to a lustful penchant for men of his race. Even so I could quickly send him into a tantrum if I failed to perceive the black significance in the American racial mosaic or said something that at least sounded like whitey insensitivity or imperviousness — even if I didn't mean it and would have done anything to retract it.

One such item was my propensity to use the phrase "in a coon's age," with which I had been familiar since my student days and which I had always thought just meant something to do with the longevity of raccoons! Well, he soon put me to rights over "coon" meaning "black," but what he couldn't do, alas, was to stop me continuing to use the expression — even after I had apologized, cried repentance, and determined out loud that the dratted words would never again escape my lips.

Whenever we met up again after an interval of many months or even years, I would break out into a cold sweat lest the coon comment materialize. Which it did. Every time. And with frequency.

I began to query my subconscious. Was it my awareness of our difference in skin hue or my liberal attempts to suppress or rationalize it that brought the dread words once more to the surface? I still don't know. But I do know that Paul eventually, after a number of years, turned it into a rather grim little joke and would grin as he berated me and called me a stupid white faggot who led a life of privileged ignorance.

Not that I want to give the impression that Paul Reid Roman (he liked the use of all three names) was ever a jolly black person. That anger, which he wore like a too-tight scarf, never left him. Not even when death called.

The night before I was to arrive in Los Angeles on a book tour I phoned him and he told me that it would be inconvenient for me to stay with him as we had hitherto planned. Instead he had arranged for me to stay with a gay couple who lived in an old, 1920s part of the metropolis that was settled with modest middle-class homes and boasted tree-lined streets.

When I arrived there it was to learn that my hosts, who were in their thirties and had been together for a dozen years or so, were breaking up. One of them in fact was to move out the very next day. In the course of that evening each secured my attention privately and bent my ear back in justification of his position vis-à-vis their foundered relationship. However, that was the smoothest part of a hellish evening.

I called Paul to inquire when I was to meet him and how he felt. (He had already suggested that he was ill, that being the reason why I couldn't stay at his place.)

Then came the anger — not directed at me but this searing time at *himself*. He railed against his sickness, declaring he had AIDS (this was before all the "HIV positive" business), and then raged against himself in a manner that tore my heart. I knew vaguely by then of the hallucinatory and kindred aspects of the disease but in this case the anger was only lit and further fuelled by the malignancy.

He refused to see me, declaring that he was unfit to be seen by anyone decent, and then raised his voice to a shouting pitch that was only made hoarse, not less in volume, by his weakness.

"I can't see you, David. Not now, not ever. I don't want to see anyone ever again. This fucking AIDS is killing me and I am ashamed. Goodbye ... goodbye."

I don't think he said any more. In any case, I couldn't have answered him. I never did see him nor hear his cultivated but plangent voice again. But I mourned him in my melodramatic way when I was restored to the comfort and commiseration of my lover, Floyd.

If our cherished bench that I hereby celebrate can take my mind to all the AIDS memorials dotted about the parks of the city, I might just as well use this occasion to address the fact of death and how it has come to inform my life. Perhaps at the outset I should say that, though the fact of living through the decades has moderated my ideas about mortality, I have mercifully never been led in the direction of the sentimental quagmire of so much current claptrap about dying and death.

My only sense of eternity is what we pass on to others through our example and influence. Indeed, that sense is what I hope animates the whole of this book and determines its contours. If we were allowed to return to fertile dust instead of the barren soil of cremated ashes, then I would like to think that we also give nurture to the bushes and trees, the wind and the rain, the soil and animal dung that was kneaded into our beings at birth. But denied that, it is only our vital informing inheritance that we can give back as mere particles of all we have absorbed during our time on this planet. The rest, the dead flowers, the weeping and gnashing of teeth, or the clenched-teeth wakes by those we leave behind, is only a solacing fancy for the living remainder of the world we knew.

Anything beyond the proper medicine of mourning I regard as specious, preposterous, and of substantive value only to the undertaker and the florist. I have come to believe that Paul's anger over so much, including his brutally quickened departure, had its roots in both his inherited genetics and the sore sad route from his ancestors' slavery to the world he found himself in. It was a weight that could only be softened by the sweet-sad song of the Negro spiritual, the caustic humour of the black comic, or Paul's bold snarl at the inequities thrust upon us.

The anger I express here is the ineluctable fruit of privilege and also probably of plain old luck. Its genesis is a fear that civilization might be regressing and that medieval boils of superstition and fear of disease and death have broken out all over again and are in dire need of lancing. It is thus a different rage from Paul's and I count it a privilege to have seen the power and persistence of his while cultivating my own.

I cannot leave the site of our bench in Jericho Park without stressing how idyllic the view is from sitting there. First the gentle slope of grass, the odd willow tree leading to the small ornamental lake bordered by a small forest of bulrushes with their chocolate bars atop their stems arising from the lake's marges, waving in the stubborn breeze that chafes the duck-dotted waters. Beyond the lake or pond one can see the brighter surface of English Bay and very often a freighter or two at anchor, waiting to enter one of the inner harbours of the port city. And towering above and be-yond this charming marine mosaic, the niveous peaks of the North Shore Mountains. It stills the heart and dilutes all the fret, not to say anger, that a person might bring to our bird-limed bench.

This is a place for friends and men and women whose acquaintance dates back perhaps forty years from my first life in the city. Or drawn from a younger generation, harvested from Floyd's thirty-odd years as a much-loved French professor at the University of British Columbia — and others gathered in the velocity of our partnership and professional pursuits from our elected homeland and afar comprising the nearly two hundred who gathered for our fortieth celebration, which inspired the bench in the first instance.

Since then we have celebrated a fiftieth such coming together — two Golden Jubilee parties, one in the home of a friend, Krysia Strawczynski, who was the retired deputy minister of health for British Columbia in Victoria, and another in Vancouver on the premises of the QLT head-quarters, whose founder, Julia Levy, was one of my landlords when I ar-rived in the city and in whose turreted house I began to write the very first collection of my short stories to be published, *Ashes for Easter* (1972).

So to this very day we have been, and indeed are, blessed with an in-credible number of friends on which, of course, one feeds profoundly for strength to meet the disparate challenges that seemingly never diminish in range or force as one grows older.

# 30
## ELISABETH HOPKINS

Rumour to the contrary, I do not write fictional versions of my friends and acquaintances. The truth is I even have difficulty with *reading* what is nowadays often inaccurately called historical fiction — or any variation on the genre. My one effort at even partial biography, *The Reluctant Pioneer: Building Opera from the Pacific Through the Prairies*, centred upon Irving Guttman, was a labour of love that proved painful in execution and received what I still believe to be unfair criticism from parochial media minds in Alberta who thought I was trespassing on their puny turf.

That is not to say I ever hesitate to use snippets or chunks from those with whom I am familiar as a motherlode for my novels or stories. Indeed, I am rather inclined to think that those novelists (other than science fiction writers) who protest their creative imperviousness to the human material about them are either gullible or dissembling. We need the faces, limbs, torsos; the humour, anger, grief, and grit; the virtues and vices of our friends and enemies, just as much as a potter needs clay.

Having said all that, I will now attest that in no area have I drawn closer to material at hand than with those friends I would classify as venerable. As I get older, the business of old age intrigues me more and more. And I have had the good fortune to meet one already aged woman who became my friend, and who, by her character and experience, inspired me to introduce a favourite nonagenarian character into my novel *The Moor Is Dark Beneath the Moon*, to make another such woman the protagonist of my most recent novel, *Geraldine*, and, finally, to insert some distinctly elderly female characters into a number of short stories as metaphors for the birth pangs of the rapidly evolving city of Vancouver.

The source of all this inspiration is one Elisabeth Hopkins. I did not get to know Elisabeth easily. Then no one gets to know a person twenty-five years or more older than oneself without a certain degree of nous and imagination. And both of those demand time. A signal example of what I mean occurred not too long after John Koerner, the painter, had introduced us and I had learned that she was a collateral descendant of the priest-poet Gerald Manley Hopkins and — even more fascinating to me — a first cousin to Gerard Manley Hopkins, the translator of the French novelist and Nobel Prize winner François Mauriac, one of my earliest literary heroes.

I had met Gerard, an Oxford don, pious Catholic, and frequent visitor to St. Basil's House in Notting Hill where I last lived in London. Elisabeth wasn't at all like her cousin; in fact, they were temperamentally poles apart, as the cliché has it, but the social and sanguinary connection between them provided a bond that was a good kicking-off point for our subsequent friendship.

She was already into her eighties when I met her, and had moved to Galiano Island, where she was befriended by both Jane Rule and Helen Sonthoff and started on her second and resoundingly successful career as a painter.

These, of course, were fairly instantly absorbed biographical facts, but beyond them lay the impish, stubborn, and quietly pious Elisabeth who hid like a cautious trout behind its river-girt boulder of concealment. In her case, though, it was a self-constructed edifice to protect her profound and cherished sense of privacy, which was, paradoxically, also to prove her nemesis.

Once her defences were secure she got her privacy — right up to the point where those about her and beyond tended to blot out her prior achievements and struggles and dismissed her currently as nothing more than a little old lady. This, I think, stirred Elisabeth to shock, even bite. And, by God! She had the fangs to do it.

At one time she wrote in her elegant Edwardian script to ask whether she could accompany us to Easter Mass at our Anglican church when she was visiting the Mainland. We were only too happy to acquiesce, and thinking she might be further solaced by the company of a coeval, outside the church we introduced her to Cy, a fellow octogenarian who was a regular parishioner at St. Mark's. If Cupid was lurking about our motives, then he should not have been. If there is one area in our partnership marked by signal failure I would say it is our dismal efforts at matchmaking — regardless of gender, age, or degree of amorousness evinced by either party.

In the precincts of the church, of course, it was all as it should be. Two shortish and squat bodies, with snow-haired heads and amiably smiling if grooved faces, joined slightly quaking hands and genially bared off-white dentures. And even after the Communion aspect of the Eucharist and the slow but stately walk back to their pew (where Floyd and I had insisted they be neighbours), all was decorum and yesteryear's manners. Cy politely waited to let her enter the pew, even though he had been placed furthest in.

The genteel mood persisted as we took him to his modest Kitsilano home, akin to our own, before taking Elisabeth to our place for lunch. The two elderly Christians (Cy was married to a vigorous unbeliever and thus came alone each Sunday to his house of worship) sat in the back of the car and to the best of our knowledge conferred as staid strangers, of comparable years and a shared Anglican faith, would be expected to do.

But with Cy's disappearance from the car all that ended. Elisabeth immediately erupted. "Who the hell was that old bore?" she began. Followed by, "No wonder his wife seeks escape each Sunday" — he must have told her during the drive of his marital rift — "and I certainly don't blame her. Just one long bleat about how life has treated him! How I detest these egotists that think they have a patent on misfortune! I get enough of that nonsense back there on Galiano. It's full of weepies. I avoid 'em like the plague!"

To divert her rather than anything else I interjected: "I hope you don't mean Jane and Helen, Elisabeth. They are the opposite of moaners."

"They're too full of running other people's lives to dwell on their own. The likes of that Cy, though, would be meat and drink to them. They're never happier than when bailing some unfortunate out. I think that's why I frustrate 'em. And that's the way I prefer it. Dear people, mind, I don't deny that. I've got nothing against lesbians. But I just don't need smothering with help from the likes of dykes or anyone else."

I let the subject drop, pondering fractionally on her surprising knowledge of the slang word for gay women. Maybe she wasn't so protected from the world's foibles as we'd hitherto thought. In any case, we both knew only too well how much the old girl relied upon Jane and Helen for a thousand and one little things — none of which we were going to risk her wrath by spelling out. She needed some sense of self-reliance and only the imprudent or impudent would attempt to take such a vital constituent of the elderly away from them. Was she herself Sapphically inclined? I never found out.

That was a major lesson learned, but there were others that are becoming commonplace as I myself grow a bit more ancient but were in those earlier days simply revelations. It wasn't too long before I saw glimpses of a younger Elisabeth peep from that carapace of infirm flesh and time-sharpened circumspection. Sitting in her tiny island cabin with her, when she entertained me with stories of the Colonel, her beloved but often naughty cat, or told him off if he misbehaved, I suddenly saw her as the English matron of some vast hospital chastising or ordering her nurses to do this or that. And I could also perceive the sheer terror that an august and starched Elisabeth Hopkins could instill in them in those hierarchically defined, pre–Second World War days.

Behind the wrinkles, the bent bones, and the still beautifully modulated upper-class voice of a charming painter in the primitive idiom of childlike themes such as *The Owl and the Pussycat* or her popular illustrated book *The Painted Forest*, I discerned the dusty dragon of those embattled years when women had had to fight for every step towards equality with their reluctant male counterparts.

And as we talked of the present, she would discount the new interest in her as an artist and declare deprecatingly that it was only because the media was always on the lookout for something novel and preferably odd. But I saw something else. I saw her covert pain at a world that refused to see her in full historic dimension but only as an old woman who had taken up painting at the tail end of life, even worse, who was devoid of a living, dynamic past with its own exciting amalgam of laughter and tears.

This, I then learned, was the true curse of aging for the female warriors who had won through, who had achieved a success, often through bloodied effort — only to have it disregarded, casually forgotten. When the leaden mantle of all those years reflected only clichéd images of lavender and lace. That bitter time when a hard-won individuality was pushed into a geriatric uniform of patronizing responses and the world began to say, "And how are *we* feeling today," and the "you" — the precious "you" — was denied as the sick are by the healthy and the veterans of living are reduced to the status of children.

All that and the precious fact that all human beings have both a right and a need to express their personal history are the kinds of things that Elisabeth Hopkins taught me. I give thanks daily that she did so while I could still incorporate her hidden realities into the flesh of my fiction before it was too late.

# 31

# CHARLOTTE (BETTY-JANE) CORSON

S he was Betty-Jane to most of the world, but my first editor and publisher was always known here on the Canadian West Coast by her bap-
tismal name of Charlotte. And perverse me, when in Toronto or her
later home in Kingston, insisted on the Vancouver usage — so that a stranger
would be (was!) often confused by the use of "Charlotte" and "Betty-Jane"
alternating from speaker to speaker and even sentence by sentence!

We met professionally at Doubleday Canada, but before our very first
encounter was concluded, bonds with the past, links of common interest,
and that stirring of empathy that signals friendship were already evident.

We both had a Philadelphia contact. I think she had worked earlier
for Lippincott, and although an old friend of mine had subsequently
moved to neighbouring Germantown, my very first night in the United
States, when en route to Floyd in California, I had passed on the premises of a Philadelphia church that had forever shattered movie-made images dating from childhood. In the back of my head, I guess, there were
cowboys and stetsons, ranches, lariats, and Red Indians. That was not
what St. Clement's on quiet Appletree Street, and Father Joiner, the
rector, presented.

I was there because my sponsor as an immigrant to the United States
was one of the curates, and it was Father Paul Collins who was my specific
host that Christmas season and who would see that I was duly seated on
the plane headed for Los Angeles and Floyd and his family, whom I was
about to meet for the first time.

But long before the challenge of that was my one and only dinner with the clergy of St. Clement's in the Octave of the Holy Nativity. I don't really know what I was expecting — the brief glimpse of sedate Philadelphia, with the warm red brick of Independence Hall and the hallowed Liberty Bell, had firmly put all thoughts of sage brush and milling cattle lowing on the open range from my mind.

But I certainly wasn't prepared for that sedate and elegant dinner table with its plentitude of silver at each place setting, adjacent to crystal finger bowls with gardenia blossoms floating in them. And, greatest shock of all, a formally dressed black retainer behind my chair with others behind those of the soutane-clad priests. Only when this formal choreography of black and white persons had come to motionless silence did Father Joiner embark on his sonorous and extended blessing of what was to come — namely lavish course after course accompanied by the presumably germane wines. And this wasn't, repeat wasn't, Christmas Day but the next one — so to freshly British me, Boxing Day. Nor, let me add, was there a hint of leftovers!

It was Philadelphia that Charlotte and I shared — not the domestic trappings of that eastern Episcopal church where during my so brief stay I heard the late President Franklin Delano Roosevelt, albeit himself an Episcopalian, referred to successively as Al Capone, Joseph Stalin, and the Republic's proto-traitor, Benedict Arnold.

But cities are really only bonds if you have shared the sweat and the quotidian life of them. And I never did get to know that eventual satellite of New York as well as I did its subsequent sister satellite, Boston, at a later date. What we *did* share was the overall publishing scene that existed in all three cities during the 1950s and 1960s — indeed, up to the point where New York City cast such a shadow that to some degree, the literary activity of the other two places began to cool and shrivel. I sit in Vancouver and know from that East Coast experience — whatever the opposing shrieks and naysaying — that some degree of isolation is healthy for the arts. Cities create their own cultural vortex and are justifiably jealous of the demographic space around them they need for constant refuelling for both bums on seats and some minimal social structures for the creators: the authors, painters, and composers.

At a personal level (I am saving the act of writing to last) Charlotte and I were to discover after a few evenings of civilized revelling that we both had a passion for pets. Dogs, of course, but very special in her life was a tamed, house-trained, and well-travelled rabbit. I could say similar things about my badger, Giulietta. It is hard to nail down this shared trait and too facile to suggest it is spurred by being childless as we both were.

"Being doggy" — at least in my book — embraces ideas over animals sharing life with us that extends far beyond canines and felines and is a substitute for nothing. Some of the happiest people I have ever met have opened their lives to pets as well as to people. One such is my younger friend whose parrot has shared his pillow and his life for over a quarter of a century and has learned to reciprocate by becoming housetrained like Charlotte's pet rabbit.

Of course, I have met people who "owned" pets — mainly dogs and cats — whose motives were wholly dissimilar from those I use as the link between my editor and myself. With such persons I have seen every reason for possession from boasting of an exotic breed, extension of a personal lust for power, implementation of misanthropy, a sop for psychological deficit, and craving for company that fellow humans have denied. Every foible, in fact from dog as gun to dog as teddy bear solace for mental distress. Poor pets!

I am no psychologist and certainly cannot see the connection, if such exists, but the Charlotte who was also so supremely patient with her pets had an extraordinary editorial patience with me that I have found with no other whose task it was to criticize my fiction and improve its final presentation in my books. From the outset she met my prickly defence and insistence that those pages of my manuscript of *No More into the Garden* that she felt might be improved should stay as I'd written them.

Chief among her objections was my extensive use of such expletives as "fuck," "shit," and the like, which I defended as authentic usage for my characters. She countered with the argument that excessive use diluted their force. In the end her wisdom prevailed and my fiction was improved — but that would never have come about, I believe, had she fought me with spirited argument and obduracy. Charlotte's way was by suggestion and question — invariably delivered in a calm tone and an easiness of voice that steadily undid my defensiveness. I don't think she was a particularly religious person, but she certainly lived by the biblical injunction in Proverbs, "A soft answer turneth away wrath," and its succeeding corollary, "But a grievous word stirreth up anger."

Soon after that she left Doubleday and I, too, went to other publishers. But she remained my friend, still continued to influence me, and shared tracts of life remote from the disciplines of the printed word.

One such area is bravery. As is deafness to a composer so damaged sight is to the editor and publisher. Charlotte suffered continuing deterioration of her vision, causing her to resort first to a magnifying glass, then to large print for computer and email, and finally to a voice equivalent and the reliance on others, particularly her husband, to read to her. This steady descent towards blindness lasted beyond her professional career, but a committed reader, wedded to print, doesn't suddenly surrender the habits and joys of a lifetime and find succour in acoustical equivalents. Yet never did I hear Charlotte grumble. Never did she offer more than a wry observation of what life had dealt her, a joke about the pits of her circumstances. But behind that was the anguish, the frustration, the need for reliance on the part of one of the most independent human beings I have ever met.

That is what I call bravery. That, since the inception and growth of our friendship and my witness of her intrepid example to deal with the unimaginable, has stirred me over and over again to attempt to emulate her singular courage.

# 32
# HELEN SOVILJ

One of the gentlest and diabetically largest women I have ever known was Helen Sovilj. She could also dismantle pretension with the facility of a squirrel cracking a nut, but I doubt whether she was ever aware of doing so. Her method was the most effective one: a total lack of pretension in herself. Oddly enough, when I first encountered her, there was a great deal of her life, social status, and Slavic background of which I was not only ignorant but would never have guessed.

First, I knew her as the on-hand owner of Angelica's, a restaurant on Vancouver's Fourth Avenue and named after the youngest of her daughters. For several months that was all I knew about her, but our relationship had already started to develop. I do not know whether Helen was widely read, but very soon she was inquiring of my life as an author and actually stuck the covers of my last two books on the wall above where Floyd and I were accustomed to sit. Shades of the Left Bank, it occurred to me with considerable pleasure, vainly comparing myself with the illustrious patrons of the literary cafés of their Parisian day.

Helen's sensibility to the arts was not confined to me. The recent works of Jack Darcus, who was then primarily a painter, were also allotted a specific place that he frequented. In other words, though totally unconnected, Jane Rule's indigenous literary salon began to have a culinary counterpart, also in the west part of the evolving city. For the cultural historian that must have its own significance, but meanwhile other developments, darker ones, were gathering over the little Kitsilano restaurant and the headland of Point Grey.

The latter is surely best known as the location of the University of British Columbia, but it also boasts the rather posh street of Drummond Drive. At the top of this was where an English professor friend lived – as a result of his wife's bounty. And Helen, I was soon to learn, inhabited the lower end of this avenue of large and spaciously grounded properties – with her three daughters and her husband, Vlado Sovilj, a surgeon who specialized in children.

He was shortly to be assassinated. Vlado was shot to death on his way to the old YMCA where he habitually played chess on Friday nights. He was murdered on September 23, 1977, a Friday. A near-hysterical Helen told me through her tears that she was quite sure Tito's secret police, the Ustaši, was responsible. Its motive, she told me, issued from a widespread rumour in the Slav community that her Vlado was to be appointed consul of a newly independent state that was about to be set up, following the looming disintegration of Yugoslavia.

I do not think there has been a specific verdict over Vlado's murder to this day. It still hangs as an obscene cloud over the history of Vancouver and the puny likes of me. It cannot hang over his devoted wife because she, too, was taken prematurely from us. But I move too quickly ...

Their eldest daughter was soon to become a doctor herself and leave for Northern California's Napa Valley. But Floyd and I were to witness the nuptials of one of the two younger girls in the felicitous gardens of their home. One of those weddings deserves comment here if only as offset to darker and more dire things to come.

We were all happily assembled, friends and relatives, on the lawn, awaiting the arrival of the minister to officiate. But as the minutes ticked by it became ever more obvious that something was wrong, that he was destined not to appear. Given what had already occurred within that family, the absence loomed even darker than it might otherwise have done. Everyone there, of course, was profoundly aware of Vlado's bloody death, and I sensed hysteria latent just beneath the surface. So did someone else, I think, for a young man suddenly stood up and volunteered to find a person to solemnize the wedding. He vanished almost immediately, and the rest of us strove mightily to fill the unwonted hiatus.

In a mercifully short space of time the youngster returned with a clerical-collared gent in tow. It was the minister himself who provided the explanation for his presence. He was a Baptist pastor attending a World Council of Churches meeting at the University of British Columbia. Between sessions he and some colleagues were taking a walk along the beach when the member of our wedding party arrived on his bike. The young man on the bike gasped out the story of the sadly interrupted wedding, and our new guest was moved immediately to volunteer to be stand-in officiant.

And what a superb job he did, making pleasantries of his unfortunate ignorance of the marriage parties and choosing words of truly apt sympathy and understanding. Situation saved; joy all around!

My final note on dear Helen becomes sombre again. More than sombre. Ominous in the light of her partner's demise. It was one of her daughters who broke the news to us. Her mother had gone back to her native land for a visit. No motive supplied. However, she had been there but briefly, driving over familiar terrain, when her car suddenly (mysteriously?) was involved in a collision with a large truck. Helen was killed instantly.

I refuse to this day to accept those bald facts as not concealing more. There is no proof, there cannot now be such proof, but Helen herself had planted suspicions of the Gestapo mores of the Ustaši vis-à-vis her husband that will haunt me always.

# 33
# IRVING GUTTMAN

Irving Guttman may have been born in Chatham, Ontario, and raised in Montreal and thus perceived on all counts as a dyed-in-the-wool Easterner. But as a seasoned novelist writing of the vagaries of the human condition, let me proclaim that all stereotypes came to an explosive end when Irving sortied west out of both Upper and Lower Canada. My novel *The Moor Is Dark Beneath the Moon* particularly specializes in some pretty outstanding characters. None more singular, though, than my friend Mr. Guttman. He is in fact a novelist's nightmare!

This totally unexpected young man with a yen for opera ended up contributing substantially to the Canadian cultural mosaic in the western cities of Winnipeg, Edmonton, and, supremely, Vancouver — as an absolute if unwitting destroyer of all facile generalizations and the very antithesis of every cliché in the book!

Jewish to the core, he is the most unracial person I've ever met. He speaks as slowly as unhurried molasses, and in temperament as an opera director he is as calm, reassuring, and measured as others are brimming with tantrums. Tell it across Canada — opera singers, musicians of every rank, actually *love* him rather than fear him. That alone is *Guinness Book of Records* stuff!

His influences upon me have been twofold: one personal, the other professional. Like a number of our friends, Irving came to us on the wings of opera, Floyd's obsession since childhood and consequently a major element in our life in terms of people and performances. When Irving asked me whether I would consider writing his biography I knew that apart from the fact we'd been friends for a number of years — he again was one of my personal coincidences in that we both first visited Vancouver in 1959 — I could always fall back on Floyd's encyclopedic knowledge and expertise of the world of opera if, at the personal level of struggling to evoke the distinct complications of Irving, I should start having difficulty.

In the spurious clarity of hindsight I can now say that my misgivings as a biographer, let alone of an infinitely complicated subject such as Irving, and again, of the fact that I was attempting to depict someone in mid-career who was still to develop his artistry and as a human being, proved fully justified.

By dint of gritted teeth, an almost daily renewed resolution, scores of interviews, and above all, genuine affection for my friend, I managed to get something of the elusive him down on paper. But I learned during that arduous year that I really had no natural gifts for the biographer's craft and that to embark on a project where the subject was both a friend and still to develop was folly. What saved *The Unlikely Pioneer* from disaster was mainly a combination of the sheer excitement of Irving's professional accomplishments, his personal charm (which even I could describe without difficulty), and Floyd's unswerving assiduity in providing the historical operatic data and depiction of the overall world of North American opera that Irving worked in over the last half of the twentieth century.

In the nearly twenty years since *The Unlikely Pioneer* was written I have come to know and love another side of Irving. That is the retired opera director who has had his fair share of sickness and that special anguish that is born of the illness of a loved one, especially a life companion — to use the synonym for lover favoured by some recipients at the Academy Awards festivities in Hollywood.

This later Irving — though always the opposite of a hard man — has been softened yet more by such experiences. Whereas in the course of professional or social business he always asked solicitously about the welfare of others, he now makes it his total concern. If ego has never bruised his relationships with singers and the like, it is now simply a warm centre of the man, inviting one's own questions as to his health and feelings.

Wryness still serves his reflections on life and the antics of his fellows, and his loud, slow generating rumble of a developing laugh is still music to one's ears. He makes me feel protective of him only at one level, and that is at the scarcity of weapons he has at his disposal to deal with the challenge of age as more and more time is left on his hands when he is private and alone. He is not, by my standards, a great reader, and although he relishes the pleasures of nostalgic looking back at the highlights of his operatic career, there are limits to the solace that cassettes, old film, and TV tapes can provide. He plays bridge — but that requires the presence of other people, which isn't always forthcoming.

He is, of course, not only blessed with a loving companion, but also, I am convinced, more professional friends and well-wishers in the world of opera than the vast majority of his peers have. And the true nature of that latter benison — that you reap what you plant — is not only exemplified in Irving but what he has implicitly taught me to strive for over the years of observing him as I have struggled to do likewise with my friends and acquaintances.

Although I have witnessed my fair share of those who, through age or illness or both, have become embittered with the accumulation of years and prone to misanthropy and the rejection of all social obligation, I have also seen the Irvings of the world as a welcome counterbalance. You don't have to be a sentimental subscriber to silver linings to discover that the rude and crude fingers of fate can, in fact, gentle and soften the spirit and provide a compassion for others that was never there before.

This isn't something that is susceptible to some kind of neat social mathematics or a factor open to a rationalization that can provide theories or doctrines that will improve the sum of human happiness. Even worse would be the notion that suffering and setback are the necessary fuel for human improvement. That form of masochism is no better than the kind of phony comfort too often dispensed by religious spokesmen addressing the loved ones of those who have been involved in tragic accidents, drawn-out and painful illness, or death.

As a novelist I draw upon the likes of Irving and other friends, such as the married couple who have faced sustained parental illness, their own physical frailty, a residual demented father, and loss of work opportunities with the concomitant worries — and still emerged as unvanquished and positive people. But the novelist in me is amoral. I have also derived inspiration from a scientist friend who contracted AIDS, turned on a world he perceived as unjust, and left this earth from Palm Springs screaming imprecations and hate for those he had cause to love most.

There are times, I must admit, when I come close to shame for my easy use of human material — from character to predicament — wherever and whenever it has entered my orbit. But I am ultimately unrepentant. "Close" to shame is all it will ever be, as my commitment to the art of fiction attains fanatical proportions and in the context of creative lodestones knows no restraint. Would I murder or maim, injure or perjure for my art? Patently not, as such actions would put my own writerly existence at risk and there could thus be no gain. This is the ugly side of all human creativity and therefore of me. I see no good purpose in gainsaying it. Just thank God for the Irving Guttmans!

# 34
## BILL REID

I had something in common with Bill Reid. With Adolf Hitler for that matter. All three of us became involved in an aspect of nationality that might not necessarily have happened. Austrian Hitler became associated primarily with Germany for most of his evil career. I have tended to play down my London ancestry and affirm my Cornishness. And Bill Reid, whose father was an American hotel-keeper decided eventually to lay claim on his mother's semi-Haida inheritance.

I have learned a lot from Bill – not all of it congenial to the politically correct brigade – and not all of it complimentary to him. I have always felt a basic sympathy with the Native Indian people of the West Coast as a result of my Cornish sensibility and awareness of the overwhelming and, at times, crushing English presence.

I bring that awareness and comparison very much to light in the last chapter of my novel *The Moor Is Dark Beneath the Moon*, where I write as follows:

> That got him thinking, and when they finally stood in the sturdy breeze, not dissimilar from the one he had left behind on the Cornish coast, he began to open up to a waiting Ken. "I suppose you could call the Cornish the equivalents over there of the Coastal Salish and the others. The English have fucked up their place just like what's happened here."

Ken smiled. His inclination was to warn about being too simplistic, but his instinct told him his lover wouldn't appreciate such a caution. "Well, I'd never thought of it that way. But I guess if you're a First Nations type and knew about your previous life as a hunter and fisherman and now lived around somewhere like today's Vancouver you could be pretty pissed off by what's happened."

Davey mulled over that. "Salmon's disappearing. Sturgeon's harder and harder to find in the Fraser River. Local abalone's gone. Those huge geoduck clams, they're on the way out, aren't they? Not to mention our forests, the few remaining groves of Garry oak. And that's just a handful of disasters, and for every one of them I can give you a Cornish equivalent. With the total death of the Cornish language thrown in to boot! And who doesn't think that the Native languages aren't on their way out around here?"

I have heard Bill Reid as both optimist and pessimist over his mother's quasi-people. Then in the course of our brief and stormy collaborations when I helped him on the scripts for his documentary films, directed by the so patient Nina Wysnicki, he veered violently between hope and despair — with the latter the rather more frequent. In fairness I must add that in his latter years, Bill was a victim of Parkinson's disease, which not only affected his artistry and craftsmanship per se, but also required medication that subjected him to rapid mood changes and sometimes sexual hyper-awareness, which was especially embarrassing for his womenfolk.

I first met Bill, a big man, prone to short sentences that were interlarded with expletives, through the CBC when I was doing a lot of freelancing, writing documentaries, interviewing, and writing the occasional radio play. He didn't much like me then, I thought, and he didn't much like me twenty years later when he was regionally famous and keen to make films of his carving and his people and reluctantly accepted Nina's suggestion that I write the scripts.

In a perverse way, I rather enjoyed his antipathy. As my published reputation grew I tended to see more of those who enjoyed my work — the detractors staying in the background or at least mute in my presence. Not that Bill disproved of my work; he was simply indifferent or unaware of it! It was the personal me that irritated him and I never did bother to find out why exactly. Being gay didn't help, I'm sure of that. I know that his film director's asking me to collaborate was born of rather odd circumstances. Nina was nothing if not honest and soon told me why she had called and asked me. She no longer felt safe alone in a room with Bill and wanted another person present — even a gay man! She also freely accorded that his persistent randiness might have been stimulated by his medications for the Parkinson's — but that, of course, didn't make it any easier for her.

If part of Bill Reid's public portrait was phony that hardly made him a rarity in my experience. Nor did it diminish in any way the power of his craft in translating Haida legend into sculptured wood. He was a great carver — though one shouldn't forget that like many of the medieval masters behind him he was strongly beholden to his helpers and apprentices who often finished the execution of his works.

If Bill knew and grew in his knowledge of the Haida, he also brought into this later preoccupation his knowledge and experience of the larger arena that he had already experienced as a jewellery maker and broadcaster. In this sense he was a sophisticated man of the world and not some rustic child-of-the-woods as some would imply. Although I never really cottoned to the man, I did admire his refusal to be shaped into some politically correct image that many late-twentieth-century romanticizers and glossifiers in the name of political correctness would imply. I don't think for a moment he was happy to be the man the media wanted him to be.

Then Bill is only just one more victim of the single most powerful unelected entity that shapes and colours our contemporary lives and creates giants from talent still on kissing terms with competence: the multimedia. Emily Carr has been so distorted locally by it that reality has been left behind. In similar vein, Margaret Atwood has been turned into a grotesque literary version of some 1930s Hollywood movie star. Broadcasters such as Peter Gzowski have been ludicrously promoted as epochal giants who have changed the face of Canada — and competence is daily paraded as genius, or at least as belonging in some cultural Valhalla that simply doesn't exist.

The perniciousness of this media inflation is that it feeds an already febrile Canadian nationalism. At the same time it allows its excess to succour an undue negativity and cynicism that with equal fatuity promotes the belief that all here is second-rate and that all Canadian reputations for quality are spurious.

Having worked for the media and been subject to both its blows and its blandishments, I have no hesitation in saying it needs overhaul. As the democracies once had to struggle to disconnect Church and State, it now must do likewise with the visual and print estates. A tough goal but since when has a betterment been achieved without struggle?

# 35
# GEORGE WOODCOCK

S ome friendships are comparable in movement to the passage of the planets: the components move closer and more distant at different times. Such was my relationship with George Woodcock and to some extent with his wife, Inge.

George was one of the few people I first met in Canada (Ethel Wilson was another) whom I had read before my arrival and who subsequently became friends. George was something of my mentor and literary "buddy" in our West Coast estrangement and shared antipathy over the eastern mandarins of the world of writers.

Not that we wouldn't both make exceptions when the author from east of the Rockies became a friend or demonstrated an awareness of new voices and new stirrings that were on a par with anything to be found in either Upper or Lower Canada. In this sense George was the quintessential professional with his instincts and tastes honed, I believe, by his adherence to an unpopular doctrine (anarchism) while many of those he admired most were far removed or at least impervious to such a position.

We first met as fellow freelancers for the CBC back in the 1960s but soon developed social patterns so that we were in and out of one another's houses regularly. Despite the disparity in our ages — he was my senior by fourteen years — and the fact that he was born in Winnipeg and me in London, we both shared a minimal interest in birthplace per se, and the bonds of a British heritage before I immigrated to Canada and he returned. We also retained British accents but, native skeptics apart, I believe that he gave himself as fully to the literary life of his natal country as I did to my adopted one. Oddly enough, it was his wife, Inge, who I think had more difficulty in surrendering her European and adopted British past for the North American present. And that in spite of her German background. For it has been my observation that Continental Europeans generally experience far less difficulty in shedding their backgrounds compared with Brits — some of whom never seem to manage at all!

Like most of the couples I have come to know in the last forty or so years, George and Inge were mutually cherishing and a polished team when it came to both work and the world beyond. But there were negative factors, too — not between them but bruising or stunting their individual lives and careers. Inge was still of the generation (though she resented it and indeed fought against it) of the wife taking second place to her husband. So her career as a potter (which might have been something else, such as a painter or a sculptor) was ever subordinate to George's as a writer. It may only have been symbolic, but her kiln was down in the cellar, and for the past twenty years or so of their life together abandoned completely.

But then George didn't always fare well from her ebullient, courageous, and stubborn personality. One icon that has always stayed with me from our almost weekly visits together was one that regularly surfaced whenever George was tempted to venture down memory lane. He and I both knew similar aspects of wartime London, I as a sailor in the Royal Navy, George as an anarchist draft dodger and writer with his German-born wife in tow. We both became familiar with the more seedy aspects of Soho, its pubs and denizens. Given half a chance we would be chuckling over mutual memories of the likes of Nina Hamnett, a disintegrating minor painter who could always be found pissed in the French Pub — and when I say "pissed" I mean literally, with a stream of urine flowing from beneath her skirt across the worn linoleum floor. Or our very different experiences of Sir Herbert Read, or again, the general ambience of the Fitzroy and the French Pub in those frowsy days of blackout, rationing, and the black market against the lethal backdrop of V1 and V2 flying bombs and rockets that prefaced the final two years of the Second World War.

Inge detested these mutual reminiscences — not for George's excluding her; he didn't — but because she loathed looking backwards.

Not for her the sepia'd charm of nostalgia, of people and places in a past world. Then not for her, old photographs, or any talk of someone writing George's biography — a threat that would bring her into instant opposition.

Sometimes she would fall back on her Buddhist beliefs to defend her attitudes but I have never been convinced over that. Inge was a woman of glorious inconsistency (one of her traits I loved most) and any religious belief could be bent or discarded if the mood and situation suited her. She loudly proclaimed her detestation of being photographed (again summoning her Buddhist beliefs) but there are nevertheless some charming photos of her and George extant that must have somehow mysteriously escaped her prohibitions.

She was consistent, though, over battling against George's wishes for certain things. I know, for example, that he would have liked an Anglican burial clothed in the majestic language of the 1662 Book of Common Prayer. I know, too, that he was not displeased (as his spouse most definitely was) when the then Douglas (later George) Fetherling proposed writing his life, which appeared subsequently as *The Gentle Anarchist: A Life of George Woodcock*.

Another thing I shared with George as well as an enthusiasm for summoning up past experience (without which appetite this book would have been an impossibility!) was a period of bleakness that forbade excessive evocation between friends. Mine was my imprisonment as a seventeen-year-old for allegations of sexual soliciting in a public toilet; George's the excessively bleak and arduous time he and Inge spent near Victoria when he returned as an adult to Canada and they both had to struggle, literally, with bare hands to make a subsistence living. In a sense they had been lured into emigration by phony and inflated promises of what they would find. So apart from the sheer drudgery they experienced I suspect there was also a shaming irritation that they had been taken for a ride.

Fortunately, things began to slowly amend after that, though bitter memories always coloured their thoughts about Jack and Doris Shadbolt, who helped them to recover from their poverty-stricken predicament and left them always uncomfortable in once having been in their debt. A very human situation that!

George was a gentle person who rarely lost his cool and with his unflappable patience would have been a good exemplar for me had I the emotional means to emulate him. But love him as I did, we were really poles apart as human beings. There are times when a profound affection for a person can lead one to wish to be more like him or her — but George Woodcock taught me that there is perhaps greater wisdom in accepting that our differences can be our valuable bonds. I speak here of the realities of friendship but I have also come to believe that a similar truth stands behind more exclusive relationships such as in marriage or gay partnership. Certainly I know couples linked by like traits: two extroverts, two shy people, even two tall or short persons. But the opposite can also hold true, and those of wildly disparate emotional and intellectual traits can achieve a highly successful and permanent coupling.

But sometimes it is the characteristic of place rather than individual person that becomes the salient feature in someone's development and, say, artistic production. It was my conviction that George's books — even George the person — would have benefited from a more challenging social and intellectual environment than what western Canada was able to afford him during his years of residence — in spite of the great deal of travelling around the planet he and Inge did during that period. Indeed, it may have been an instinctive awareness that his imagination needed more that took him to other countries.

Of course it is an unprofitable enterprise to play the "if" game with a friend's life and I have no evidence that had George remained in London, say, or gone to the volatile climate of New York City, he would have gained greater focus in intellectual enterprise and gone deeper in his analyses and assessments of the human condition. But I do asseverate as an attentive observer that he spent far too many hours with folk of lighter intellectual displacement and of rather more frivolous disposition and that they constituted a substantial waste of the writer's time. I think there were occasions when he suffered from being too big a fish for the pool in which he swam and that he duly paid a price for reigning in a benevolent hell rather than serving in a more challenging heaven.

That is a price that we must all risk if we insist in living and working away from the major centres. If I say I don't believe it has harmed me,

I still have to admit that the thought has pricked me from time to time throughout my career. But finally, the George I knew and admired was a stolid reality, sufficient unto himself. I loved him and learned from him for what he was and not for what he might have been. He still awaits further biographical treatment to take us in evaluation and scope beyond Fetherling's pioneer work. However, the pessimist in me doubts whether he will ever get it.

# 36
# TENNESSEE WILLIAMS

I f this is little more than an anecdote it is included because it nevertheless contains a specific and what I consider a heartening message. I met Tennessee Williams but once in my lifetime and that for a space of less than three hours! At a dinner party in fact. And there were six of us around the table. It was out at Lions Bay on the way to Squamish and Whistler, in other words a few miles north up the coast from Vancouver where the view of Howe Sound is spectacular and the actual drive there in my opinion equal to the Grand Corniche along the Mediterranean or Highway 1 through Big Sur along the coast of California, south of Monterey.

The playwright had permitted his latest play, the one-actor *The Red Devil Battery Sign*, to have its premiere in Vancouver. The year was 1981 and the reason for his presence and his play's initial presentation arose from his much publicized conviction that "they [the critics] wanted to get him" and that his recent dramas would thus also fall victim to the Broadway vendetta that awaited any new work of his. (A small irony, certainly not lost on me, was that the play had a poor reception here, too.)

His attitude was what one read in articles and books, heard on radio, and saw on TV. Namely, that the playwright, though brilliant and the hugely successful author of such plays as *A Streetcar Named Desire* and *The Glass Menagerie*, was wholly paranoid about the reception of all his work. And that was also very much the opinion of the voluble, somewhat diminutive author sitting next to me. Then there was so much of this voluble gay genius from the Deep South that came through the scrim of media presentation as wholly familiar: his wry sense of humour, his absolute refusal to play the role of a literary celebrity or famous figure, and his birdlike peeping at this person and that as he took them in and digested their presence. Our hosts were the journalist Max Wyman and his wife, Susan. Max is one of those rare newspapermen who is neither brash, cocksure, nor noisy in proclaiming his territory and knowledge. His quiet attentiveness, which was equally neither sycophantic nor at all self-conscious, obviously appealed to Tennessee — so that by the time he and I met, the distinguished playwright and short story teller was relaxed and quite happy to be his unarmoured self.

I have interviewed scores of high-profile personalities in my time as well as knowing several others socially, but Tennessee Williams stands out as one of the most unaffected I've ever met. He could rid one of any sense of dealing with a "personality" and quickly find a common ground where no one need be perpetually on guard.

A precise example of what I mean occurred at the dinner table. Sitting between the dramatist and myself was the young man who had accompanied him and who had been variously described as his chauffeur, his secretary, and his companion. Whatever his functions may have been, he was intent on shielding his employer from an excess of social intimacy and would frequently interrupt any interrogation by one of us of Mr. Williams. Before the latter could open his mouth and offer some languid response in his relaxed Southern drawl, his factotum would begin, "Mr. Williams doesn't feel," or perhaps, "Mr. Williams believes"— but this business didn't last very long. In the closest I saw Tennessee come to exasperation, and even then most mildly, he suddenly exclaimed, "Oh, for Christ's sake, Danny [or whatever], stop interrupting people. And cut all that 'Mr. Williams' shit. I'm Tennessee to everyone here."

From there on his conversation speeded up and the tone was consistently relaxed. I should add that Tennessee was careful to see that it included the young man and he constantly referred to him to verify an impression or to contribute an opinion.

There is of course a convention of Southern politeness that at times can obscure reality rather than just soften it. But I think Tennessee Williams would have been seen as a polite man had be been born in Brooklyn or spent time as a Parisian waiter! That compounded the evening's social success — but so did his willingness to discuss his work (past and present) and, equally important, the lack of obsequiousness on the part of the other diners. He and I spoke of the role of appropriation in the creative enterprise and of the possible gay advantage in entering the shoes of womanhood or someone of a different coloured skin.

As with so many Americans who are not governors of border states on the other hand, he had little or no sense of the country he was in. He was very impressed with the beauty of his immediate surroundings and expressed himself at length of the fact. But we could have been dining in Alaska or Albania for any sense of cultural or political difference for him. The unifying strand, I think, was the distance from New York City and the geographical gap between him and his enemies occupying the theatrical positions of power in that place.

In fact, after a delightful visit to his personal past, a naughty reminiscence of eminent others, or a question about our local theatre world and genuine-sounding questions about our personal lives, it invariably seemed that his paranoia would ultimately reel him in and back to his normal contours of self-awareness. It was a kind of glue, I decided by the time it came to shaking hands and saying our goodbyes, that held him together. Although it was couched in pain and indignation, punctuated by these periodic outbreaks over being hard done by all those theatre vultures who sought his professional and personal downfall, his paranoia was in fact his lifebelt. He couldn't have survived without it!

# 37
# CAROL SHIELDS

We've all been bit by death, fashioned the scars it leaves us in
its wake.

Carol's demise a further rut along the potholed path we
humans needs must take.

We fling warm thoughts to those who harbour ice be-
queathed by those who've gone.

In this case, Don, her husband, friend, and father of her
five-leafed womb.

A mawkish national press recites distress and cites a string
of books.

But I recall an elfin face and voice of fragile eggshell force.

In forty years my Carol never veered from steel concealed
as gauze!

(This generous partisan of women's clay who, dying, sent
me "cover quotes.")

So rightly claimed by gender as for female rights she fought,
She stayed a prickly radical, uncomfortable with gains.
With success she took a mansion but it became a fort.
Ill at ease with all awards, she giggled at her fame.

*Then Carol was an artist, her catholic interests serviced by unerring words,*

*So in the end, refusing tags, she fled confining boxes that others would confer.*

I wrote the above sonnet just a day or so after I heard of Carol's death, which was not, of course, unexpected. She had been suffering from successive bouts of cancer for several years concomitant with her retiring with her husband, Don, to Victoria and purchasing their final home, which might possibly be described as a mansion. Ironically, of course, this "retreat" to Victoria and the onslaught of illness necessitating spells in hospital with debilitating chemotherapy was more or less simultaneous with the final and extensive burst of international recognition, including her winning the Pulitzer Prize in the United States.

Sickness and plaudits were also accompanied by her last novel, *Unless*, and that, too, met with yet more paeans of praise here in Canada, from her natal United States, and from the United Kingdom — to name but three of her literary constituencies.

My relationship with Carol Shields was different from what I have had with most fellow authors. For one thing she treated Floyd and me as a due couple, hyphenated in our affection and loyalty and therefore deserving of a mutuality. Without that, of course, I cannot extend full friendship with anyone. But in Carol's case it was more profound than just an observance of social niceties, however crucial the latter might be. She had a genuine respect for my partner's mind and learning and it is not coincidental or mere politeness that his name appears amid the author's thanks at the back of *Unless*.

Nor, may I say, was her attention turned to Floyd only when his French or academic prowess was called for. Carol's respect for anything never contained the constituent of subservience, and for the forty years I counted her a friend (which began with her husband at the University of British Columbia and continued through their association with the University of Manitoba), she always manifested a high sense of the civilizing value of universities in the general community. No, she simply perceived my lover in the fullness of his person. Then, unlike some, Carol Shields didn't go about cutting couples in half and seeing them only as half sections.

She had a comparably unified sense of her own tribe of writers. Intellectuals of a general cast also, for that matter. She looked at each four and square. She expected people with brains to use them, those with ideas to express them, and those with verbal fluency to implement their gift ably, whether in speech or in writing.

That reminds me of a small anecdote relating to the four of us one springtime morning shortly before her death. Husband Don was about to take Floyd to the French conversation class that he ran for a local senior citizens' group, to show him how it worked and whether Floyd thought it might be improved upon. As the two left that spacious and by no means overfurnished house, Carol turned to me, indicated the sun-washed conservatory where we could sit, and said in a tone she might as well have used over the quaint mores of their neighbours in the French village in which they owned a house, "Now, David, let's sit down and discuss Mortality." Which was precisely what we did in the welcome early sun's warmth pouring through the surrounding glass.

This wasn't just because she found the matter personally pressing but because I had earlier mentioned my feelings when Floyd had entered hospital with his subsequently removed cancer and she thought we had not covered the topic adequately. It was that, I think, that was indicative of Carol's whole way of thinking. She was always the inquirer, always wishing to know and discover anything and everything — from the most obscure grammatical usage to the most arcane elements of life itself.

Which leads me to another key factor about this signally attractive writer that had a profound effect upon me. I mention in the above sonnet just how tough under her soft-voiced, very feminine mien Carol really was. And that toughness in the form of sheer resilience and persistence marked both her character and her art. Her conversation was littered with questions but it was also healthy with opinions. And her writing enjoyed the spillover from fluid life to the permanent page.

She always was what I have also striven to be: a penetrating writer who, without being a show-off, demonstrated a wisdom and psychological acuity that rewards readers with a bonus to the sheer pleasure of her excellent style and the excitement of meeting a vivid and extensive imagination.

Another of her literary gifts that I likewise seek to emulate is the ability to encompass or embrace more than one single constituency. To be sure, Carol Shields is a woman's writer — just as I cannot escape being a gay one — but for both of us, that has to mark a beginning, not an end. In fact I think it was her absolute confidence — mastery, if you like — of the terra femina that allowed her to address other persons, other places, so that she ends up with a catholicity of response that a less concentrated author might not have. I have yet to meet a man, straight or gay, who has said they found her work off-putting because of its feminine emphasis. That, of course, is why she was so drawn to the similarly talented Jane Austen and was compelled to write a book about her.